TEXAS WOMAN'S UNIVERSITY

295616

**Date Due**

| | | | |
|---|---|---|---|
| DEC 12 1973 | | | |
| | | | |
| MAY 0 6 1988 | | | |
| | | | |
| | | | |
| | | | |
| | | | |
| | | | |
| | | | |
| | | | |

BRO
DART Printed In U.S.A.

# JAMES THOMSON (B.V.)

# James Thomson (B.V.)

## A CRITICAL STUDY

## Imogene B. Walker

~

**GREENWOOD PRESS, PUBLISHERS**
WESTPORT, CONNECTICUT

*Copyright 1950 by Cornell University Press, Ithaca, New York*

Reprinted by permission
of Cornell University Press

First Greenwood Reprinting 1970

Library of Congress Catalogue Card Number 70-108847

SBN 8371-3738-1

Printed in the United States of America

LIBRARY

B↸T

295616

7↸↸

4-12-71

# Preface

MY initial impulse to write this story of James Thomson (B.V.) sprang from my disappointment at the failure of previous works, even those contributing most to the knowledge of the poet, to consider adequately the significant relations between the man and his literary productions. The H. S. Salt biography, invaluable especially for factual material, first gives the data of Thomson's life and then considers his writings by categories, thus not only divorcing the two but also obscuring the chronology of the works. Bertram Dobell's "Memoir," printed as an introduction to *The Poetical Works of James Thomson, B.V.,* and his *The Laureate of Pessimism* both err on the side of brevity, giving too little information concerning the life. None of these three gives as full an understanding of Thomson and his works as I believe is possible; much less do such studies as James E. Meeker's *The Life and Poetry of James Thomson (B.V.),* Josefine Weissel's *James Thomson der Jüngere, sein Leben und seine Werke,* William Maccall's *A Nirvana Trilogy,* or even the best of this group, Jeannette Marks's chapter on Thomson in *Genius and Disaster.*

[ v ]

# PREFACE

This study, then, is the attempt to gain that understanding by the exploration and elucidation of as many relationships as possible. To this end I have considered the influences on, events in, and conditions of Thomson's life; his honest, analytical, philosophic cast of mind; his sympathetic and imaginative temperament; his works both as outgrowths and as evidence of the above; and the development and final statement of his philosophy. This philosophy, as expressed in his writings, is the result of his life, his cast of mind, and his temperament, plus the times in which he lived (the reader's knowledge of which I have assumed). These five strands I have endeavored to weave into a whole that the relations between them may become apparent, letting first one and then another dominate as chronology dictates.

My work on this study has been lightened and made pleasant by the co-operation of members of the staffs of the Huntington, the John Crerar, and the Newberry Libraries, by the help of the Secretary of the National Secularist Society in London, and especially by the assistance of Mr. Percy Dobell, who made available to me unpublished notebooks, diaries, and letters. To Mr. Dobell for his generosity in permitting me to use these documents and to quote from his father's works and for his later kindness in reading, correcting, and criticizing an early draft of this work, my debt is indeed great. The kindness of the following publishers in granting permission to quote from their publications as listed is appreciated: King's Crown Press, *The Catholic Apostolic Church*, by P. E. Shaw; Yale University Press, *The Life and Poetry of James Thomson (B.V.)*, by James Edward Meeker; Watts & Co., *The Life of James Thomson ("B.V.")*, revised edition, by H. S. Salt.

[ vi ]

## PREFACE

Professor Benjamin H. Lehman of the University of California, whose criticism has been as constructive and severe as his patience has been long, is also deserving of more gratitude than I can well express. And finally I owe sincere thanks to Professor Franklin Walker of Mills College for his unflagging encouragement and his unfailing confidence.

I. B. W.

*Uppsala, October, 1949*

# Contents

# JAMES THOMSON (B.V.)

# CHAPTER I

# "Doubt and Fear"

## 1834-1862

IT IS with London that the name of James Thomson (B.V.) is most closely associated, for it was in London that he lived most of his mature years and produced most of his work. London periodicals published most of his writing; London publishing houses issued his books; and London, to a large extent, stimulated him to write "The City of Dreadful Night." Yet Thomson was already twenty-eight years of age when he came to London in October, 1862, and already a writer. He had had some half-dozen pieces of prose printed and almost twenty poems; in addition he had a still greater bulk of unpublished poems, many of which were printed in the course of years.[1] Little of this early work showed more than mere promise; as a writer Thomson still had much to learn. But if he was not yet a mature author when he came to London, he was an adult, a man. And on this man various influences and events had left their irradicable stamps. His cast of mind, analytical, philosophical, and unswervingly honest, had been molded. His

---

[1] Bertram Dobell, in *The Laureate of Pessimism,* p. 11, noted, however, that Thomson destroyed much of his early work in later years.

temperament, alternately gay and moody, always sympathetic and imaginative, was already apparent. His philosophic development had passed through its early stages and its future direction was clearly pointed. To understand as fully as possible Thomson's mature writings, those which have gained his reputation for him, it is necessary to go back to the years before he came to London and examine the influences and events in order to determine just what stamps they left, observe the early evidences of his cast of mind and his temperament, take note of the beginnings of his philosophy and try to explain them.

Concerning Thomson's parents and early childhood, little factual material is available, just that contained in a letter of autobiography written to his sister-in-law in the last year of his life and the few details added to this account by H. S. Salt in his *Life of James Thomson ("B.V.")*.[2] The father, James Thomson the senior, a native of Pitlochry and the son of a Scottish weaver, was a sailor who attained a good position in the merchant service. He was a cheerful and companionable man who enjoyed reading and reciting, liked music, and was fond of singing with his friends. A contrast to him was Sarah Kennedy, whom he married in London in January, 1834. She was a deeply religious young Scottish woman, whom her son remembered as "more serious, and pious too" than her husband, "mystically inclined" and with "a cloud of melancholy overhanging her." They were nevertheless very happy together when the elder James was home from sea and enjoyed their modestly comfortable home and their children, James, born on

---

[2] This letter is quoted at some length by Salt in the *Life,* 1889 edition, pp. 3–5. Subsequent references to Salt's *Life* in this study are to this edition except as otherwise noted.

November 23, 1834,[3] and a daughter, born three years later.[4] (The second son, John, was not born until 1842.)

In 1840, however, this pleasant home life was disrupted. The father returned from a voyage, suffering from paralysis which seriously affected his mind as well as body. For a year he was subject to mental instability and his temper was unpredictable and disagreeable. That the year left a deep impression on the mind of young James, then but six years old, is indicated by the fact that forty years later he remembered such a detail as that his father had taunted his mother because she was the elder of the two. But in time the instability settled into permanent weakness of mind, and the man turned from his happy friends and songs to embrace a somber religion.

The immediate result of the illness was, of course, financial difficulties. It has been said that these were made even more acute by the father's intemperance; but there is no evidence of such a failing except a comment reportedly made by Thomson many years later that intemperance ran in the family: "Nearly all the members of it who 'had brains,' especially a gifted aunt of his, fell victims to its power." [5]

By 1842 the family had moved to London's East End. His parents no longer able to support the boy, an old fellow townsman of his mother gained admission for him to the Royal Caledonian Asylum. Certified to be in good health, he entered a fortnight after his eighth birthday and, as it turned out, just

---

[3] "James Thomson, mariner in Port Glasgow, and Sarah Kennedy his spouse, had a lawful son, born November 23, 1834, and baptized February 28, 1835, called James." From old parish registers in the Register House, Edinburgh, quoted by Salt, *Life,* 1914 edition, p. 1.

[4] The daughter died of measles at the age of "about three," according to the autobiographical Thomson letter. Thus at the time of his father's illness Thomson was the only child.

[5] G. W. Foote, "James Thomson: I. The Man," *Progress,* April, 1884.

before his mother's death, when the dissolution of the family was completed by the removal of the infant John, born in 1842, to the charge of a Glasgow aunt. Thus came to an end the first period in Thomson's life.

The details of these eight years are so meager as to make difficult any generalization. Yet one, inadequately emphasized I think, can safely be made: a strong religious atmosphere pervaded the home. That this was important in the boy's life is apparent from the several references to religion in the autobiographical letter. Thomson's mother was a devoted Irvingite; he spoke of her having followed "Irving from the Kirk when he was driven out," of her draping Irving's portrait with yellow gauze, and of her books by Irving on the interpretation of prophecy, which he read. The religion of Edward Irving was somewhat less austere than that of the strict Calvinists, for he early rejected the theory of the "elect" and embraced the doctrine of the universal love of God.[6] On the other hand, it was a much more emotional religion; he encouraged, even preached, the theory of charismatic Christianity. It was, as a matter of fact, because he gave free reign to glossolalia during services that in May, 1832, he was declared "unfit to remain minister of the Scottish National Church" in London.[7] When the doors of the church were thus closed to him, he and his followers, among them presumably Sarah Kennedy, formed the new church which in time became the Catholic Apostolic Church.[8]

---

[6] A. L. Drummond, *Edward Irving and His Circle*, p. 110.

[7] *Ibid.*, p. 210.

[8] Since there is but one sure date connected with Thomson's mother, that of January, 1834, when she was married in London, it is impossible to state positively that it was at this time that she followed Irving from the Kirk. It may have been to Irving's dismissal from the Church of

The services of the new church give a good idea of the temperament of those who followed Irving.

> One in particular looked very wild. His face was flushed, and he occasionally turned up the whites of his eyes in an ominous style. . . . Just as Irving reached the point I have mentioned . . . the elder . . . burst out in a sort of wild ejaculation, thus: "Taranti-hoiti-faragmi-santi; O ye people—ye people of ye Lord, ye have not the ouches —ye have not the ouches—Ha-a-a." . . . When he began, Irving suspended his exposition and covered his face with his hands. As soon as the voice ceased, he resumed the thread of his discourse, till the "tongue" broke out again "in unknown strains." [9]

In addition to such regular services, there were many private meetings at which the "gifted" spoke in "tongues." In writing of Irving during this period, Carlyle commented, "For many months he has been puddling in the midst of certain insane jargonings of hysterical women, and cracked-brained enthusiasts. . . ." [10] It is very probable that Thomson's mother was among the hysterical women.

Of the nature of the father's religion after he became paralyzed one is less sure, for Thomson's remarks do not in-

---

Scotland as a minister and as a member in March, 1833, that Thomson referred. Because, however, after his dismissal as a minister from the Scottish National Church in London he formed a new church, whereas after his dismissal as minister and member from the Church of Scotland he merely returned to his congregation in London, the reference is probably to the earlier date.

[9] Account of eyewitness quoted by P. E. Shaw in *The Catholic Apostolic Church*, p. 50.

[10] Thomas Carlyle, *Reminiscences*, p. 298.

clude the statement that the man embraced his wife's faith. He wrote merely, "He used to take me to chapels where the members of the congregation ejaculated groaning responses to the minister's prayer, and to small meetings in a private room where the members detailed their spiritual experiences of the week." It is highly probable, however, that he did become an Irvingite; the description of the meetings in the chapels and private room are compatible with descriptions of the Irvingite meetings. But whether the father joined his wife's church is comparatively unimportant. The significant point is that during his first six years Thomson lived in a home wherein religious emotionalism was high and that this emotionalism was intensified during the two following years. Certainly such an atmosphere left its mark.

The child's acceptance by the Royal Caledonian Asylum rescued him from this mentally unhealthful environment. The Asylum (now called the Royal Caledonian Schools) was founded in 1815 for the purpose of "supporting and educating the children of Soldiers, Sailors, and Marines, natives of Scotland, who have died or been disabled in the service of their country, and also the children of Indigent Scottish Parents resident in London, not entitled to Parochial relief." Early accounts of the planning of the institution state explicitly the aims of the school and indicate to some extent the course of study. Since the school was "for the purpose of bringing up the children in habits of industry, it is proposed to introduce into the establishment certain manufactures and mechanic arts, adapted to their subsequent pursuit in life. Due attention is also to be paid to the morals and religion of the children." "With the Caledonia Asylum is to be connected a Gaelic Chapel, where Divine Service is to be performed in the ancient Language of

Caledonia, and in the English Language alternately." The boys were to be taught "reading in English and Gaelic, Writing, and Arithmetic." [11] There is not, however, any evidence that Thomson learned even a word of Gaelic. [12]

Little Jimmie remained at the Asylum for almost eight years, a happy boy, apparently, leading an emotionally more normal life than he had known in his own home. He was described during those years as high-spirited, recognized by his companions as their leader and by his teachers as an unusually quick and alert student. [13] He showed ability in all his studies, but especially in mathematics, an aptitude which foretold the logical analytical quality that was to be an outstand-

---

[11] For information concerning the Royal Caledonian Asylum I am indebted to the headmaster of the School in 1935, who generously lent me printed matter from the historical files of the institution. This matter consisted of the following items: "History of the Institution," *Aberdeen Daily Journal,* Monday, December 23, 1901; "The Royal Caledonian," *The Temple Magazine,* date unknown, prior to 1903; account of the meeting of the Highland Society of January 10, 1809, telling of the original planning of the Asylum, name of publication unknown, dated January, 1809; "The Royal Caledonian Asylum," *The Teacher,* May 2, 1908; " 'B.V.'," *T.P.'s Weekly,* March 10, 1905; "The Royal Caledonian Asylum, Bushy, Herts: A Home and School for the Children of Scottish Parents," *The Child,* September, 1912; "Caledonian Asylum and Chapel," *The Courier,* Saturday, July 9, 1808; brochures for 1929, 1934, and 1935 for the Royal Caledonian Schools, Bushey, Herts, which give historical data as well as current information concerning the school.

[12] It is probable that the requirement of Gaelic had been abandoned by 1842. The difficulty of meeting it is indicated by the fact that as early as 1822 Irving, then very young and still an orthodox minister of the Church of Scotland, was inducted as ordained minister of the Caledonian Chapel only after the congregation had rented the chapel from the Asylum directors in order to circumvent the Trust Deed of the school which specified Gaelic preaching. The pulpit had been vacant for a year while a fruitless search was being made for an acceptable bilingual minister (Drummond, *op. cit.,* pp. 44–46).

[13] Salt, *op. cit.,* p. 6.

ing characteristic of his mind in later years.[14] And he acquired, in addition to the fundamental academic training, at least a slight education in music.[15] A love of music, perhaps started by his father's songs and thus fostered by the school, remained important throughout his life; even when he was most pressed for money in his later years he managed to go to the inexpensive popular concerts, and he used the theme of music from the earliest to the latest of his works.[16]

But this happy, carefree life could not continue indefinitely. The boy wished to become a clerk in a bank or a mercantile office; but training for such an occupation entailed a period of unsalaried apprenticeship and was therefore impossible for a lad with neither money of his own nor a family to back him. His teachers recommended the profession of army schoolmaster. The suggestion did not appeal to him; but since he could think of no other practical solution to his problems, he accepted the advice and on August 2, 1850, entered the Royal Military Asylum, then at Chelsea, as a monitor.[17]

By this time his high spirits, emphasized in accounts of his years at the Royal Caledonian Asylum, had given way to a gentle seriousness. The daughter of the William Grays, with whom Thomson spent his holidays each year for a decade and who tried as best they could to be father and mother to him, wrote of the boy that he was "wonderfully clever, very nice-

---

[14] Bertram Dobell, "Memoir," *The Poetical Works of James Thomson,* *(B.V.),* I, xiv. Subsequent references to Dobell's "Memoir" in this study are to this edition.

[15] Salt, *loc. cit.*

[16] "To a Pianist" (also titled "To Arabella Goddard"), 1859, to "He Heard Her Sing," 1882.

[17] Salt, *loc. cit.*

looking, and very gentle, grave, and kind." [18] The family knew no cause of this new graveness, but it was probably an indication of early maturity induced by recognition of the necessity of becoming entirely self-dependent financially.

But the "gentle, grave" manners of Jimmie were not such as to keep him from being popular with his companions at the military school. At the same time he was, as he had been at the Caledonian Asylum, a good student and continued to show special talent in the field of mathematics. The greater part of his intellectual enthusiasm, however, he gave to his own reading. When he was fifteen, Byron was his favorite; the next year it was Shelley. Swift, with whom he was later compared, Fielding, Smollett, Defoe, and De Quincy, who influenced him especially in his early work, the boy read eagerly and admired greatly.[19] Perhaps he dipped into Shakespeare; one cannot be sure.[20] Thus at an age when the average boy finds reading but dull schoolwork, Thomson was discovering

---

[18] Account given by Mrs. Agnes Gray Greig, quoted by Salt, *op. cit.*, p. 8.

[19] Salt, *op. cit.*, pp. 6–7.

[20] If Thomson did not read Shakespeare at this time, he certainly did later. George Saintsbury's comment in his review of *The City of Dreadful Night and Other Poems, Academy,* June 12, 1880, ". . . we cannot help wishing that Mr. Thomson had read Shakespeare more and Leopardi less" is somewhat misleading since it seems to imply that Thomson's acquaintance with Shakespeare was only casual. Thomson did know Shakespeare; and while, according to Salt, *op. cit.*, p. 287, he did not frequently quote the dramatist, he did so do on occasion, according to G. W. Foote, "James Thomson: I. The Man; II. The Poet," *Progress,* April and June, 1884. Moreover, in a letter to W. M. Rossetti, dated August 5, 1872, Thomson wrote that when he went to America "the only books I could find room for in my portmanteau were the Globe Shakespeare and Pickering's diamond Dante (with Cary's version squeezed in for the notes and general assistance)."

many authors who were to give him enjoyment throughout his life, to act as touchstones in his literary criticism, and to be his masters and inspiration for his creative work.

On August 5, 1851, after a year at the school, Thomson was sent to Ballincollig, Ireland, about five miles from Cork, to continue his studies and to gain practical experience as a student teacher. There he was immediately accepted into the home of his supervisor, Joseph Barnes, who was pleased equally with the friendliness, wit, and good spirits of the lad and with his unusual abilities as a teacher. And Mrs. Barnes, no less delighted with the seventeen-year-old boy, mothered him with a care he had not known for years.[21] Into this home, the first he had known for nine years, he slipped contentedly. After such a length of time at boarding schools, he was especially appreciative of the sympathy and domestic peace afforded him by the new friends and the new environment. Nor was his appreciation a superficial, sentimental one forgotten as soon as he left the Barnes; ten years later, in 1862, he addressed a series of six sonnets to them expressing his sincere gratitude for the happiness they had given him.[22]

During the eighteen months Thomson was at Ballincollig he formed a close friendship with a private soldier of a regiment stationed in the village—young Charles Bradlaugh, only a year older but already an embryonic reformer, filled with self-confidence and boundless ambition, who was beginning to be known in small circles as an atheist and a radical. At the time there was nothing to mark the relations between the two young men as of special importance, but the friendship was to last twenty-four years and to influence to some degree,

---

[21] Salt, *op. cit.,* pp. 8–9.
[22] Printed in the Dobell "Memoir," pp. xvii–xx.

I think, Thomson's thinking, to affect the events of his life, and to direct, obliquely, the form of much of his writing. The name Bradlaugh recurs repeatedly in Thomson's story.

In this same year and a half Thomson met and fell in love with Matilda Weller, a beautiful girl of fourteen, and soon became engaged to marry her. It is difficult to understand such a relation between these two even when it is remembered that at eighteen Thomson was already a man earning his own living.[23] Yet Salt, in commenting on the improbability of such an engagement, wrote in 1889, "There is evidence in existence which proves beyond all doubt that the facts . . . are substantially correct." [24] He did not, however, offer the evidence and it is now lost. Dobell wrote, somewhat more conservatively, "Whether there was any formal engagement . . . is not clear; but it cannot be doubted that it was well understood that Thomson, after a sufficient lapse of time, should claim the young girl for his bride." [25] At any rate when Thomson went back to Chelsea on January 16, 1853, to finish his course of study at the Military Asylum, his expectations for the future were bright. With no ambition to acquire wealth or aspiration to achieve prestige, his hopes, simple and commonplace, were merely for a pleasant and serene family life, such as he had known with the Barnes at Ballincollig, with an affectionate wife and loving children.[26]

---

[23] There is some slight confusion concerning his age at the time. Salt, *op. cit.*, p. 13, wrote, "Thomson could only have been in his eighteenth year." Dobell, however, in *The Laureate of Pessimism*, p. 5, stated, "Thomson had not yet reached his eighteenth year." In the earlier "Memoir," p. xxiii, he had written, "Thomson . . . was scarcely eighteen years of age."

[24] Salt, *op. cit.*, p. 13.

[25] Dobell, "Memoir," p. xxiv.

[26] The expression of Thomson's desires for a simple family life oc-

Six months after his return to Chelsea, he received word of Matilda's death on July 19, 1853. Critics have made much of the effect of the bereavement on Thomson's life. Dobell, for example, wrote in the "Memoir," "It may therefore be taken as certain that the death of Matilda Weller was the chief cause of Thomson's unhappiness. . . . I believe that if she had lived to become the wife of Thomson, he might very well have got the better of his melancholy disposition. . . ." [27] Salt commented, "We are compelled to believe . . . that it was the death of this young girl that, above all other single circumstances, fostered and developed the malady to which Thomson was predisposed, and that in this sense, at least, it was the cause of his subsequent despondency." [28] In other words they felt that, had Matilda lived, Thomson would probably have overcome the melancholy tendencies they believed he inherited from his mother and might not have succumbed to the dipsomania they considered a legacy from his father. [29] And they were supported in their view by the fact that at times, as in the unpublished poem, "I Had a Love," Thomson himself agreed with them. [30]

Possibly their assumption is correct; at least it cannot be refuted. On the other hand G. W. Foote, an intimate friend of Thomson in the latter part of his life, asserted that Matilda

---

curs at intervals throughout his work but especially in the early poem, "The Deliverer," 1859, and in section xvi of "The City of Dreadful Night," 1874.

[27] Dobell, "Memoir," pp. xxx–xxxi.

[28] Salt, *op. cit.,* p. 16.

[29] I find no evidence whatsoever except that slight bit cited earlier that Thomson's father was a heavy drinker, yet the belief that the poet's dipsomania was inherited was widespread and unquestioningly held by his friends and by many critics.

[30] For discussion of "I Had a Love" see Chapter IV.

was "merely the peg on which he hung his raiment of sorrow; without her another object might have served the same purpose." [31] And Jeannette Marks reasonably suggested that, even under more favorable circumstances, the development of Thomson's dipsomania would probably not have been retarded to any degree and that two lives instead of one would then have been disastrously affected.[32] With these two latter critics I am inclined to agree, for certainly Thomson's low spirits were a basic part of his character. If his melancholy had been capable of being easily dispelled, if it had not been deeply rooted in his nature, surely his grief for Matilda would have worn itself out while he was still a young man and he would have found happiness with another girl. Nor, as the assumption seems obliquely to imply, did Thomson fail because of his loss to struggle with all his strength and will against his weakness; one questions whether anyone could have helped him wage a better fight.

It will be noted that the above critics have considered the importance of Matilda's death somewhat negatively, as what might or might not have happened had she lived; and in so concentrating their attention they have apparently failed to examine thoroughly certain positive evidence on which sound speculation may be based. Such an examination brings to light three important, and completely ignored, points. The first is simply that this was Thomson's first experience with death which can be assumed to have had any deep significance for him. It is true that he had twice before suffered bereavement, first of his sister and later of his mother; but the sister had died when he was a child of five and the mother when he was

---

[31] G. W. Foote, "Preface," *Satires and Profanities*, p. viii.
[32] Jeannette Marks, *Genius and Disaster*, p. 94.

only eight, away from home at his new school in a new environment with new interests to distract him from his sorrow.[33] Thus these two losses could not have given him comprehension of the implications which lie in the experience of death. Ten years later, however, he was a man, a man whose thoughts were of the future. At such a time death held for him a deep and philosophic meaning. Full of hope, he was made to realize with a sudden shock the uncertainty of human existence. The plans of his life were smashed in an instant, and he understood the vanity of human wishes. Man, he discovered, is an impotent creature. That he learned the lesson well is evinced by the fact that it came to be one of the major tenets of his philosophy. And he first expressed it in "The Doom of a City," written in 1857, four years after Matilda's death.

The second neglected point is Thomson's attitude towards his love for Matilda as expressed especially in the poetry of the decade following her death. Matilda, he wrote, was so "holy-pure" that only spiritual love was worthy of her. Physical impulses were gross and lustful, to be eradicated if possible, at least to be repressed. Thus in "Love's Dawn," written in the year preceding Matilda's death, Thomson in speaking of what may reasonably be assumed to be normal sexual desires called them "my heart's caged lusts." In the guise of Bertram, in "Bertram to the Most Noble and Beautiful Lady Geraldine," 1857,

> . . . subdued
> Beneath thy pure calm noble maidenhood,

---

[33] Thomson's father died in 1853. Because they had been separated for the preceding eleven years and because for the two years prior to the separation the father had been mentally unbalanced, his death can reasonably be assumed to have had little significance for Thomson.

he rejected the physical aspects of love. And in "The Fadeless Bower," 1858, he regretted not that his love should never have been consummated but rather the loss of his

> . . . dream that we should stay
> Entranced in unfulfilling bliss.

But the clearest expression of the attitude is in "The Deliverer," 1859, where, having described the virtues of woman, he continued:

> Chastity, purity, and holiness
> Shall shame thy virile grossness. . . .

From these various expressions it is clear that Thomson felt the physical elements in his love unworthy, perhaps even shameful. Nor, it should be noted, was this an attitude of brief duration; the poems in which it is expressed were written over a period that began in Thomson's eighteenth year and extended into his twenty-fifth. And, although he then ceased writing about the attitude, there is nothing to indicate any change in it.

Because information concerning Thomson's early years is so meager, no explanation of his feeling towards the sexual aspects of his love can be more than a mere guess. Possibly the feeling was the more or less normal worshipfulness of the idealistic and romantic youth. Possibly it was the result of his religious training, either at home or at the Caledonian Asylum, but there is no clear evidence to support this view. But whatever the cause of this feeling, its very existence throws light on certain aspects of Thomson's later life and at the same time offers a reason why he continued, almost to his death, to write of Matilda. There is no question that he romanticized his love for the girl or that, although he was in no other respect sentimental, he nourished his grief, writing of it, thinking of it, probing the wound when it showed signs of healing. The golden-haired sweetheart appears and reappears in his poetry and prose. There are references to her (though in justice to Thomson it must be noted that there are not many) in letters, in diary entries, and in reported conversations with friends. And this insistent preoccupation with the memory of Matilda was, I am convinced, a defense against sexual urges, a defense he needed because he felt them shameful and wrong, perhaps even evil. It is this attitude, I believe, which explains his failure to marry.[34]

---

[34] Of any interest which Thomson showed in women following Matilda's death there are but two stories, neither of them authenticated, both questionable. The one is dated late in his life and is left for comment till Chapter V. The other is dated 1860. This concerns Helen Gray, the elder daughter of the earlier mentioned William Gray. Salt quoted, *op. cit.*, p. 40, an account written by Mrs. Greig (Agnes Gray, the younger daughter) concerning a visit Thomson made to the Gray home, during which he was "painfully silent and depressed" and after which they never again saw or heard from him. In attempting to explain such actions, Salt referred to an earlier incident, also recorded by Mrs. Greig, quoted p. 8: "Whatever Helen said or did won approbation from him. . . . Previous to going (to Ireland) he earnestly requested that my sister might be allowed to correspond with him, a request which my parents thought it wiser to refuse." Salt then continued, "It is possible that Thomson's discontinuance of his visits to Mr. Gray's house after 1860 was due to a revival of his early affection for Miss Helen Gray, with whom, it will be remembered, he had earnestly desired to correspond, and who was now engaged to be married. It is known that he still treasured many years afterwards a purse which she had worked and given to him; and it is noticeable that among his early poems there is one named 'Meeting Again,' which is dated September, 1860, and may perhaps refer to this occasion."

James Edward Meeker, in his *Life and Poetry of James Thomson,* 1917, amplified the story without, however, indicating his authority for so doing. His account, pp. 48–51, runs thus: "It must be remembered that before going to Ireland, Thomson had been quite intimate with

## DOUBT AND FEAR

The third point I wish to make concerning the importance in Thomson's life of Matilda and her death deals with the religious difference between the two young people. The earliest evidence that there was such a difference is found in the above

---

Helen Gray and had corresponded with her. In September, 1860, when he called on the family he found her engaged. . . . Yet there was another element in his attitude which brought on melancholy during his stay at their home, and which probably caused his unexpected silence afterward. This was a brief but intense revival of his early love for Helen Gray, which is shown in the sad and obviously sincere *Meeting Again:* [twelve lines quoted]. Thomson was thus torn between two impossible affections—one, that life-long and passionate reverence for the dead Matilda, and the other, this rebirth of an earlier love for a woman already engaged to marry another. It is only natural that Thomson should have tried to put Helen Gray out of mind, for she could not be his, despite the pathetic hope of his melancholy poem," etc.

An examination of the circumstances of the whole episode indicates weaknesses in the Meeker account. At the time Thomson requested to be allowed to correspond with Helen, he was at least three months short of seventeen, since the request was made before his departure for Ireland on August 5, 1851. In a letter to Agnes, January 6, 1860, quoted by Salt, p. 36, Thomson commented that Helen was "some three or four months over twenty." Thus at the time he went to Ireland, she was eleven. Granted that Matilda was but fourteen when he fell in love with her, I still cannot conceive that he was so deeply in love with Helen as to justify Meeker's expression, "an intense revival of his early love."

Nor do I find that analysis of the poem supports the story. The first three stanzas, starting with the line concerning the parting, "Your eyes were burning with wild love and woe," are a little exaggerated to refer to an eleven-year-old girl. The fourth stanza contains lines contrary to the facts of the situation:

> We are allowed to meet,
> And mingle henceforth all our sighs and tears
> While these two hearts shall beat:

In the fifth stanza the idea of being possessed by woe and sin seems strange applied to Helen. The seventh stanza deals with Thomson's weakness, foulness, and evil, words which he frequently applied to himself when writing of Matilda. And the eighth stanza is concerned with a vague companionable oblivion. Thus I cannot accept Meeker's story without knowing his authority for it.

noted "Love's Dawn," written while Matilda was still alive. In it he shrinks from her eyes,

> Piercing the cavernous darkness of my soul,
> Burning its foul recesses into view;

> .    .    .

> The cynic thoughts that fret my homeless mind,
> My unbelief, my selfishness, my weakness,
> My dismal lack of charity and meekness.

It is suggested again in "Tasso to Leonora," 1856:

> Yet foul demons in my ear
> Hiss most wordless hints of fear,—
> That this hideous dream's wild strife
> Is our soul's substantial life!

> .    .    .

> But, you cannot scorn me, Dear,
> Though I sink in doubt and fear?

And it is implied throughout the major portion of the auto-biographical "Vane's Story," 1864, but most obviously in the lines spoken by the girl (Matilda) to Vane (Thomson) when she speaks of his "unbelief" and his "wicked godless lifetime's course." From these passages, and from other hints in Thomson's early poems, one infers that Matilda enjoyed an unquestioning, orthodox faith, that she was perturbed that her sweetheart felt any doubts, and that her distress made Thomson unhappy. At the time the difference was, in all probability, comparatively unimportant; but after the girl's death it assumed an emotional relevance which will be considered later.

During the year following Matilda's death Thomson continued his studies at the Royal Military Asylum at Chelsea. In about July, 1854—the exact date is unknown—he finished his work there; and on August 7, 1854, two and a half months before his twentieth birthday, he enlisted as a schoolmaster in Her Majesty's Army, where he remained until discharged for a minor infraction of rules October 30, 1862.[35]

The eight years Thomson spent in the service were externally dull and uneventful, marked only by trivial day-to-day occurrences and changes of station.[36] In the story of his development as a poet, however, they have, in my opinion, much more significance than has been recognized. A careful consideration of the first signs of his dipsomania, his prevailing moods (so far as they can be determined), his intellectual activities, and the early development of his philosophy in this period permits a better understanding of Thomson and his works.

Least well documented is his dipsomania. According to Salt, "Intemperance . . . was unknown to him up to about 1855; but from that date onward he gradually became liable

---

[35] The story of Thomson's discharge, so far as it is known, is very brief. In 1862, while stationed at Portsmouth, he went up to the military post at Aldershot to visit a friend also in the service. In the course of his stay there a group of men, of which he was one, went swimming in a pond where swimming was forbidden. When an officer demanded the names of the men in the party, he was refused and "further altercation" followed. Subsequently, a court-martial was held, and on October 30, 1862, Thomson was discharged from the army (Salt, *op. cit.,* p. 47).

[36] A full factual account of Thomson's army career, including lengthy quotations from many of his letters, is found in the two editions of Salt's *Life of James Thomson ("B.V.")*. Less complete accounts, with a few different details, are included in Dobell's "Memoir" in vol. 1 of *The Poetical Works of James Thomson* and in his *The Laureate of Pessimism*. The list of posts at which Thomson was stationed is as follows: 1854–1855, Plymouth; 1855–1856, Aldershot; summer 1856 to early June 1860, Ireland; June 1860 to spring or summer 1861, Aldershot; spring or summer 1861 to May 1862, Isle of Jersey; May 1862 to October 30, 1862, Portsmouth. More accurate dates are not available.

to its power. . . ." [37] Dobell commented, in the "Memoir," "It is possible, indeed, that the jovial good-fellowship which is one of the chief characteristics of life in the army may have done him some harm by developing that tendency to excess which was a fatal defect of his temperament. . . ." [38] And later he wrote, in *The Laureate of Pessimism,* concerning Thomson's discharge from the army in 1862, "His great infirmity had, I believe, already begun to show itself. . . ." [39] These are the only references to the beginnings of Thomson's dipsomania, but, slight as they are, they establish adequately its start during these years in the army.

Concerning his prevailing moods, however, there is more evidence. An examination of the extant poems written during these years indicates that he spent much time brooding over the loss of Matilda. Of the thirty-six, fourteen, or better than one-third, deal with Matilda and love, a much higher percentage than he wrote on the theme in any other similar period. His translations of the Heine poems are undated and it is not, therefore, possible to use his selection as evidence. Yet among those he translated at some time, three are on the subject of a dead sweetheart and may have been done during the years he was in the army. But even discarding them as evidence, it is clear that he spent more time than was emotionally healthy grieving for the girl, giving in to his sorrow. And in so doing he constructed an emotional form for Matilda, retained to the end of his life. She is almost invariably the pure girl who, had she lived, would have rescued him from the desert of life and made a better man of him. Even the first part of "I

---

[37] Salt, *op. cit.,* p. 24.
[38] Dobell, "Memoir," p. xlix.
[39] Page 18.

Had a Love," written twenty-five years after her death, might be taken for one of his early poems were it not for references to the passage of years.

A second major mood was that of dissatisfaction with himself and his life. Despite the fact that he was a successful teacher he found his work lacking in stimulation.[40] For the most part the men he had to teach were phlegmatic, without either curiosity or interest. Convinced that were he a better instructor he would somehow inspire them with the desire for knowledge which animated him, he considered his teaching a dismal failure and blamed himself for his students' dullness. With a despair more sincere than indicated by the tone of the jingle, he wrote to a friend of the life of an army schoolmaster:

> . . . he thinks of how he lives,
> With a constant tug and strain—knowing well it's
>     all in vain—
> Pumping muddy information into unretentive sieves:
>     . . . and he might
> Fix sound bottoms in these sieves, too, were he not
>     so weak a man.[41]

A natural manifestation of this dissatisfaction with his work and himself was a vague but intense restlessness. At one time he considered deserting from the army to go to sea.[42] At another, when he was stationed in Ireland, he was inordinately excited by the rumor that his regiment might be transferred to Australia. Its sole interest for him was that it was far away; to go to Australia, he wrote, would be "escaping from banish-

---

[40] Dobell, *The Laureate of Pessimism*, p. 9.
[41] *Loc. cit.*
[42] Salt, *op. cit.*, p. 23.

ment." [43] Even when orders came to go, not to Australia but back to England, he was stimulated simply because he was eager to move:

> When you've worn a coat a year, it begins to look so queer,
>> That you'd better get a new:
> When you've stood one place a year, it becomes so
>> dull and drear,
>> That you'd better change it too. [44]

On his twenty-third birthday Thomson gave expression to his dissatisfaction in an unnamed and unpublished poem. [45] His life was unsatisfying, a failure. He had achieved nothing: he was not wise, he was without love, he had lost his religious faith. His years were "ill-used,"

> All lost forever! and the hours to come,
>> Poor refuse! but our sole remaining wealth
> So much the likelier thence to share their doom!

They had been drab years unmarked by either heights or depths, dull years leading nowhere, stupid years without meaning or significance. Such was his "lone base flat of torpid life!" Better would be "wild drunkenness than hectic drought." In lines which echo Keats he summed it up:

---

[43] Fragmentary letter, undated, to Agnes Gray, quoted by Salt, *op. cit.,* pp. 37–38.

[44] *Ibid.,* verses quoted pp. 38–39.

[45] Dobell in the "Memoir" quotes extensively from the poem, remarking, "The biographical interest of this poem is so great that I am strongly tempted to print it in full; but I am prevented from so doing by the fact that the author, shortly before his death, desired that it might not be published, as he had then altogether outgrown the mood in which it was written. I see no reason, however, why I should not summarize its purport . . ." (pp. xxxiv–xxxv).

Flushed grapes, full-charged with life's delirious wine,
  Brush my wan temples, hanging thick about:
Chained fast I cannot reach them, while I pine
  To press their very inmost rapture out,
Flooding with fire these dust-dry lips of mine;

.     .     .

And torture breeds new tortures in the dread
That ere they fall my power to drink be dead.

He longed for a life of great physical activity to bring him a sense of satisfaction. Next best would be a life of strong emotion, from which he would emerge with experience and knowledge and a better understanding of the world. Contrasted with these dreams was his own life:

  I fret 'neath gnat-stings, an ignoble prey,
  While others with a sword-hilt in their grasp
  Have warm rich blood to feed their latest gasp.

True it is that in time Thomson outgrew the mood, but it remained with him for the following nine years at least, still strong enough to be the basic theme of the four poems "Art," 1865, "Philosophy," 1866, "Life's Hebe," 1866, and "The Naked Goddess," 1866–1867, and of the essay "Per Contra: The Poet, High Art, Genius," 1865.[46] For even as he failed to derive satisfaction from his work in the army, so, during his first years in London, he failed to find satisfaction in his creative writing.

Considering the love of reading which Thomson had earlier shown, I doubt that lack of an adequate social life in the army established the pattern of his intellectual activities; yet this

---

[46] For discussion of these works see the following chapter.

lack may very likely have influenced their extent. It was expected that, as a schoolmaster, he would not associate with the enlisted men; [47] still he was not of the officer class and did not share its activities.[48] Accordingly the number of men from whom he could choose his friends was small; and among these he found during his first two years in the service few or no congenial, intelligent companions with whom to share the long off-duty hours.[49] In an effort to fill the idle time he turned, almost immediately after his enlistment, to the study of foreign languages.[50] What aroused this particular interest is not known, for apparently he had done no work with foreign languages before; it was probably simply the desire to read certain authors in the original. At any rate he began with German, first studying thoroughly a grammar and then plunging directly into Heine, a dictionary in one hand and the poems in the other. As he read he made translations, combining his poetic abilities with his new linguistic skills. Later

----

[47] Dobell, "Memoir," p. xxvi.

[48] Salt, *op. cit.,* note, p. 43.

[49] Salt suggests, *op. cit.,* p. 20, that Thomson lacked such companionship throughout all his army years, but the letters written from Ireland, where he was stationed for four years beginning in the summer of 1856, indicate that there he found at least a few friends with whom he enjoyed interests of more than a trivial nature. Of these, the most important seems to have been John Grant. Concerning Grant, Mr. Percy Dobell, son of Bertram Dobell and present literary executor of Thomson, wrote me the following: "This John Grant may have had more influence on Thomson than has been recognized. He was an Army Schoolmaster with whom 'B.V.' was on terms of intimacy nearly all his life. I have some of Thomson's poems written out in Grant's hand. Thomson must have been in the habit of lending Grant his mss." I have, however, been unable to find any more information concerning Grant than the few passing references made to him by Salt, and these are without particular significance.

[50] Salt, *op. cit.,* p. 21.

during this period, apparently in 1861, he started the study of French.[51] In addition to his studying and translating, he read widely. Happily for him there were large libraries at almost every military station, "each having enough good books . . . to satisfy a moderate man for the year or so of his probable stay." [52] It was during these years that he developed his great admiration and respect for Browning. He also read Mrs. Browning, whom he called the "greatest of English poetesses," and Meredith.[53] And finally, of course, he worked on his own poems.[54] Thus Thomson spent most of his evenings during the eight years of his army life and, apparently, during the rest of his life, for his diaries of 1874–1881 indicate that the pattern continued the same, merely expanding to include all or most of each day. He studied, translated, read, and wrote; other activities were secondary.

But more important to the literary critic than the beginnings of Thomson's dipsomania, than his dominant moods, than his intellectual activities—more important because it

---

[51] Salt, *op. cit.,* p. 44. In the 1914 edition of the *Life,* p. 19, Salt indicates that Thomson taught himself, in addition to French and German, "Italian, and a fair amount of Spanish; also a little Latin and Greek. . . ." Of these last two languages I find no evidence either to prove or disprove Salt's statements; but concerning the "fair amount of Spanish," I am inclined to believe that Salt exaggerated somewhat, for in his "Carlist Reminiscences" Thomson commented that he spent his evenings in Spain with other English correspondents and English-speaking Spaniards. It is quite true, however, that he did teach himself Italian, but only after he left the army. So far as I can determine, he worked only with French and German during these eight years.

[52] Letter to Agnes Gray, June 27, 1859, quoted by Salt, *op. cit.,* pp. 33–35.

[53] Salt, *op. cit.,* p. 22; letter to Agnes Gray, May 14, 1859, quoted *ibid.,* pp. 30–33.

[54] The earliest dated poems extant are "Love's Dawn," 1852, and "Parting," 1854.

points directly towards "The City of Dreadful Night"—is the development of his philosophy during these years. Yet this important aspect of Thomson's story has been either completely ignored or treated in a most cursory fashion, perhaps because this early development is beclouded by the emotions which it engendered and which must be considered along with it and as a part of it. In fact much of the account of it must be made chiefly from the point of Thomson's emotional reactions.

Thomson's mature philosophy was, stated negatively, a denial of the basic concepts of orthodox Christianity. It is only natural, then, that the first steps toward that philosophy should have been religious doubts. No accurate date can be assigned to the beginnings of these doubts, although Dobell, writing of the boy's stay in Ballincollig, commented, "His opinions even then diverged a good deal from the straiter paths of orthodox belief." [55] And evidence from later poems, such as "Vane's Story," referring to events of these eighteen months supports this broad dating. Nor can the original cause, if there was any specific cause, be ascertained. It is possible, however, to point out two events which, in my opinion, at least stimulated his religious thinking.

The first of these was meeting Charles Bradlaugh. With him Thomson spent much time talking and reading. According to Salt and Dobell, however, neither made any attempt to convert the other to his own way of thinking: Thomson's ideas, losing their orthodox coloring, were in a state of flux; and Bradlaugh's, though steady and well defined in his own mind, were not yet so animated by the proselyting spirit as

---

[55] Dobell, "Memoir," p. xxvi.

they were to become.[56] Yet it is logical to think that, because of mutual sympathy, Bradlaugh wittingly or unwittingly exerted considerable influence on Thomson at this point in his development.[57] In Bradlaugh Thomson found not only a keen and receptive listener but one who must have encouraged the somewhat unorthodox ideas he tentatively put forth. That the self-confident Bradlaugh agreed with his doubts and questionings, that he went even farther and professed his own atheism, must surely have reinforced Thomson's wavering disbelief and hastened its growth. Agreement can be a potent influence. In view of the painful nature and the length of the religious struggle Thomson was about to experience, one is inclined to think that a companion as intellectual as Bradlaugh but of a firm faith might have deterred him and temporarily directed him back to the religion on which his hold was becoming unsure.

A second event which stirred Thomson's religious thinking, though less obviously than his association with Bradlaugh, was the death of Matilda, which impelled him to look to religion for the consolation offered by a belief in immortality. It was characteristic of Thomson's thought processes that he could admit only those ideas based on and supported by reason. It was also characteristic of him that his intellectual honesty made self-delusion impossible. Thus in his search for consolation he was forced by his very nature to scrutinize religion closely and logically—and he found that it crumbled under his scrutiny. That its foundations were so unstable at first

---

[56] Dobell, "Memoir," p. xxvi; Salt, *op. cit.*, p. 10.

[57] The letters written by these men during the years 1852–1856 are all lost; otherwise the extent of their mutual influence might be gauged accurately.

frightened and dismayed him; his security, his tranquillity were gone, destroyed by his own thinking. With almost passionate feeling he cried,

> Would foolish wisdom's whirls of dreary thought
> But leave my doubt-vexed spirit undistraught.[58]

From the bottom of his heart he wanted to believe in God, in immortality, in the essential goodness of mankind; but his observations of the world and the implications which his analytical mind saw in those observations abundantly fed the ever-growing doubt which bit by bit undermined, weakened, eventually killed his faith. There was in his mind and in his heart a constant struggle between belief and disbelief; for the comfort of his heart he strove to retain the faith of his early training while gradually losing it because of the strength of his intellectual integrity.

This conflict between strong emotional desires and cold reason engendered fear, bitterness, and a weariness of spirit and resulted in sincere and deep suffering. The clearest evidence of its sincerity and depth is that Thomson called his deviation from religion his "sin." Until 1864, two years after his release from the army, his work bears frequent reference to this "sin." He spoke of himself as mad with self-consciousness of guilt and woe, accurst, his breast seared with remorse, his brain gnawed on by hopeless doubt and anxiety; he felt intense self-reproach and self-scorn. Nowhere, however, did he offer any explanation of or reason for his feeling; but by gathering together scattered lines from various poems, the reader is able to understand the nature of the "sin." The clearest picture of

[58] Verses written on his twenty-third birthday.

its character is a passage from the autobiographical poem, "Vane's Story," written in 1864, in which Thomson reviews his earlier years. Although this passage is frequently quoted, its relation to his religious struggle has not been pointed out and it has therefore not had a full interpretation. The girl of the narrative asks,

> "And do you feel no bitter grief
> Of penitence for unbelief?
> No stings of venomous remorse
> In tracing backward to its source
> This wicked godless lifetime's course?"

Thomson, as Vane, responds to that plainly stated query that in former times (that is, during these early years of his life) he had indeed suffered great self-reproach for his doubts and questionings:

> "I half remember, years ago,
> Fits of despair that maddened woe,
> Frantic remorse, intense self-scorn,
> And yearnings harder to be borne
> Of utter loneliness forlorn."

This amounts almost to a statement that Thomson's "sin" was simply his doubt and his unbelief, and that this "sin" was to him the cause of deep self-scorn that he was too weak to accept the Christian religion on faith, of remorse that he did not, of despair that he could not.[59]

---

[59] Dobell followed this same line of thought briefly in *The Laureate of Pessimism*, pp. 59-60: "He was unable to free himself—or at least not till late in life—from the delusion that he was a sinner who had sinned the unpardonable sin. 'The Christian conscience,' says a discerning critic, 'survived in him to torment the sceptic.' He had in him the blood,

Thomson's use of the word *sin* in connection with his un-belief seems to me highly significant. That he suffered a sense of guilt throughout his life is apparent: it is seen in many of his poems; it is generally considered to be at the root of his dipsomania. But the reason for it is not clear, nor with evidence available at this date can a positive statement be made. It is possible, however, to give an explanation which is at least reasonable and sound in view of what evidence there remains, and the clue to that explanation lies in the word *sin*. It will be remembered that the first eight years of Thomson's life, years when being "good" or "bad" are extremely important to a child, were passed in an exceptionally religious home. The following eight years he spent in a strict Calvinistic school. Then he fell in love with Matilda at a time when he was experiencing his first religious doubts, doubts which apparently distressed her and consequently distressed him. Her death "proved" that he was wrong in questioning. Yet he continued to question, and questioning, felt guilt, guilt to the extent of calling his unbelief a sin. This theory, that Thomson's sense of guilt resulted from his deviation from Christianity, is given support by the fact that in "Vane's Story," Matilda and the "sin" are closely associated.[60]

---

tinctured with fanaticism and intolerance, of long generations of Scotsmen, who had bequeathed to him something of their religious fervour, together with their not less fervent love of the national drink. His vigorous intellect enabled him to free himself from the bondage of Calvinistic theology, but its poison could not be altogether eliminated from his system."

[60] The general line of reasoning in this paragraph was suggested to me by Dr. Charles Tidd, psychoanalyst, formerly of The Menninger Foundation. I have received additional assistance from Dr. Christine Sears, acting head of the Child Development Center, Oakland, California.

In this religious struggle there are three distinct elements. In the first place, Thomson desired to accept certain positive beliefs: that there was personal immortality and that life had purpose in accordance with a divine plan. Second, he was tormented by the doubt which arose when these beliefs were contradicted by the conclusions his intellectual honesty forced him to draw from empirical knowledge. And finally, his spirit "doubt-vexed," he felt a deep longing for the peace and rest of a quiet acceptance of orthodox Christian religion. These three closely related elements—desire to believe, doubt, and longing —one predominating one day, another the next, all welded together in a chaotic, inconsistent, but entirely comprehensible whole, make up the story of his struggle, told in various poems of the period.

Thomson's desire to believe in immortality is to be found especially in the Matilda poems, as in "Parting," 1854.[61] This is superficially a statement of a quiet and orthodox faith, but it is couched in such trite, artificially poetic language that the reader is aware of the conflict between the assertion and the underlying feeling. This conflict is emphasized by Thomson's use of italics in the second line of the last stanza, a device which tells of desperate hope rather than calm belief: "Soon again we two *must* meet."

A similar note of desire to believe is clear in Thomson's expression of his faith in a divine plan in his first philosophic poem, "The Doom of a City," 1857, which is in four parts, "The Voyage," "The City," "The Judgments," and "The Return." In section vi of "The Voyage" and section ii of "The Judgments," he states unequivocally his belief in such a plan. The tone, however, is forced, over-insistent, and the language

---

[61] See also "The Fadeless Bower" and "At Death's Door."

is not his own but that of the pulpit and the hymnbook. One feels no sincerity in the passages. Moreover Thomson is guilty of gross inconsistencies. In section ii of "The Judgments" the "Titanic forms" (who for forty lines chant examples to prove that everything is properly ordered) say: "We have never yet traced out Punishment or Reward." Yet the succeeding six sections concern punishment.[62] Finally, from the list of illustrations he uses to shore up his expression of belief in a divine plan, he excludes all which failed to support the theory, a bit of intellectual dishonesty so out of keeping with his character that it immediately casts doubt on the whole. It is impossible to feel that, however positively Thomson stated his belief in a divine plan, he did not recognize that for him it was pure sophistry.

Further evidence that Thomson's expressions of belief are properly interpreted as the results of a desire to believe rather than accepted convictions is the thread of doubt, the second element in his religious struggle, running through many of the poems. As I have noted, this doubt appeared in "Parting." It is implied later in the dramatic "Tasso to Leonora," 1856, when Tasso cries out that if life were more than a flitting dream, if things were actually as they seem, "I must be mad, mad,—how mad!" In "The Doom" the doubt is expressed symbolically as a monster,[63] and more clearly in the consideration of nature's indifference towards her "lord," man.[64] Thomson was finding that for him the logical inference to be drawn from what he saw about him was that the world was not made for man's special benefit and that he has no power over it, for it steadfastly continues its ruthless course regardless of what-

---

[62] See also section vi of "The Voyage" and section iv of "The Return."

[63] "The Voyage," section xiv.

[64] "The City," sections ix, xvii, xxi; "The Judgments," section xiv.

ever befalls him. As though arguing with himself, Thomson first hinted, then more fully suggested, and finally openly presented the unconsciousness of nature. Found in the doomed city, wherein all men had been turned to stone, was a scroll boasting that Earth had imparted to Man the dearest secrets of her treasured beauty—yet after his destruction she continued to bloom and bear fruit. In such a manner Thomson expressed the doubt that tormented his mind, inconsistent with his explicitly stated belief in a divine plan, but far deeper and more sincere.

The yearning for peace and rest, the third element in Thomson's religious struggle, was an emotion which found expression in short works, products of more or less transitory moods, rather than in a long, sustained piece of writing such as "The Doom." A definition of that yearning is hardly necessary; it was compounded of the unrest, the anxiety, and the weariness of spirit attendant on a conflict between religious convictions unquestioningly accepted in youth and the findings of science understood in maturity, and it engendered a deep desire for some sort of certitude, be it full and uncompromising religious faith or a complete relinquishment of it. Its first expression appears in "Suggested by Matthew Arnold's 'Stanzas from the Grande Chartreuse,'" 1855, in which is heard the prayer Thomson must often have uttered in the lonely nights, "O God in Heaven . . . teach us how to worship Thee!" The note of hopeless longing again appeared in the sonnet, "A Recusant," 1858, and in the poem titled only "Sonnet." [65] In the latter as in "A Recusant" he effectively created the mood of longing, crying

---

[65] "Sonnet" is undated but Dobell noted in *The Poetic Works* that it was "probably written in the sixties."

## JAMES THOMSON (B.V.)

I gaze and seek with ever-longing eyes
  For God, the Love-Supreme, all-wise, all-good:
Alas! in vain. . . .

But the most beautiful and most powerful expression of this
theme is in the little known "Mater Tenebrarum," 1859, a
thirty-line poem which seems to me the best of Thomson's
early works and the one which shows most clearly his potential
ability. The mood of yearning is so firmly established by the
closely knit structure, the careful and musical diction, and the
final climax, and so well maintained without a moment's drop
of the intensity of feeling, that even the final note of hope
takes on the color of hopelessness and does not destroy the
harmony of the whole. Despite the careful structure (which
makes use of a varied refrain occurring in the first two lines of
each of the three stanzas and builds up to a climax in the last
two lines of the poem), the whole gives the impression of
long pent up emotion suddenly released in a convulsive cry
of pain and anguish. Unfortunately, I can quote no passage
from this poem without mutilating it; one must read the
whole work to see how it epitomizes the mood.

Coming soon after the beginning of this mental turmoil,
apparently, and running concurrently with it was the second
step in Thomson's philosophic development: the search for
a philosophy of life to take the place of the Christian faith
which he was losing.[66] He was being forced to acknowledge
that the religion of the church was not for him, but he was

---

[66] The dating, admittedly not positive, is based on the evidence of
"Vane's Story," on Dobell's suggestion that Thomson's religious doubts
began while in Ballincollig, August, 1851, to January, 1853, and on the
assumption his search for a compromise did not long precede his first
expression of it in 1854.

still more protestant than agnostic. His emotional nature craved a faith; his reason denied the faith in which he had been reared. Sincerely he sought a compromise, something his imagination could grasp in place of orthodoxy, something his analytical mind would find reasonable. For approximately a decade Thomson sought a new belief, toying with some philosophies, weighing others more seriously, even tentatively accepting one or two for short periods.

The most important of these philosophies was a personal religion, not unlike Unitarianism, built shakily on what he believed to be the basic concepts of orthodox Christian faith, stripped of all the forms, both ritualistic and theological, with which the church had surrounded them. The true spirit, he felt, was clouded and forgotten. His efforts were to abstract that spirit and believe in it. As early as 1854 in "Suggested by Matthew Arnold's 'Stanzas' " Thomson had touched on this compromise. In 1857, in "The Doom," he developed it with more feeling, calling the church the fossil of a faith, the bones without blood and breath. In "The Dead Year," three years later, he wrote that some worshippers were clinging blindly and tightly to the falling temples, treading "down new reason," while others were abandoning them utterly, "and with them God and God's restraining law." In "Shelley," 1861, he lamented that because the priests were false and the shrines impure, mankind was losing faith in God Himself.[67] In all these poems he implied that, although the churches were bad, one should retain faith in God. He also made a distinction between the God of formal religion, of the church, and God as he himself believed (or attempted to believe) Him to be.

---

[67] Not to be confused with the essay, "Shelley," 1860.

The God of the church seemed to be either a monster great only in power or malice, or a phantom evoked by bewildered thought. Thomson's God was one who reigned with infinite love for all things.

This personal religion was essentially pantheistic in character, a result, probably, of Thomson's admiration for Shelley and his regard for that poet's ideas and of his own imaginative, sympathetic, and democratic thinking.[68] Thomson sensed God more easily in a gay spring flower than in a well-fed, unctuous clergyman; yet he escaped the sentimentalism that frequently attends pantheism because he was no less aware of the "beast, and worm, and plant, and slime" of life than of its more pleasant aspects. His expressions of pantheism in "The Doom" and "A Happy Poet," 1857–1859, are comprehensive, clear, and full definitions of that philosophy.

> . . . the universal Spirit rife
> In Man and Nature,—One in all their forms,
> Alike contented with its worlds and worms,
> Through all its countless masks alike resplendent,
> The Breath of Life, eternal and transcendent.

> And of the perfect Unity enshrined
>   In omnipresence throughout time and space,
> Alike informing with its full control
>   The dust, the stars, the worm, the human soul.

---

[68] In 1874, Thomson wrote, "When I was about sixteen, I fell under the dominion of Shelley, to whom I have been loyal ever since" (letter quoted, without name of recipient, or further date, by Salt, *op. cit.*, p. 7). During these years, when his interest in pantheism was at its height, he wrote two essays and one poem on Shelley and shortly thereafter he dedicated another poem, "Vane's Story," to him.

This pantheistic personal religion satisfied Thomson well enough emotionally; but unfortunately for his tranquillity, it was not equally satisfying intellectually, for it was based on the premise that there was a good and conscious god—and that premise Thomson felt was unsound. He could not find firm, logical proof to support it; he could not accept it as a fact. This personal religion was not, therefore, the answer for him, yet he rejected it with considerable reluctance, as is evinced by the fact that considerations of pantheism reappeared from time to time in his works until 1865.[69]

There is one more step to be considered in this early development of Thomson's philosophy, a significant one. The De Quincy–inspired "To Our Ladies of Death," 1861, notable for its passages of rolling music and its mood-suggesting pictures, marks a turning point. Up to the time of its composition Thomson's thinking had been largely negative: he had been rejecting orthodox Christianity bit by bit; he was finding the personal faith he had built up untenable. After 1861, however, his thinking became more positive, and "Our Ladies" points the direction it was to take in the future. To be sure, he was not yet ready to deny individual immortality, and again he expressed the pantheistic idea of "earth's general soul," though conditionally. But more and more he was seeing life in terms of laws, though he did not yet stress the attribute of unconsciousness; and he was strongly attracted by the concept of material immortality, to which he gave detailed treatment. This concept, to become an emphatic element in his mature philosophy, appealed to his imagination and at the same time

[69] Major expressions of pantheism occur in the essays "Shelley," 1860, "The Poems of William Blake," 1864, both to be discussed in Chapter IV, and "Open Secret Societies," section iii, 1865.

[ 37 ]

satisfied his intellect. The poem leaves little doubt concerning which of the ideas Thomson would drop and which he would accept and expand.

With the writing of "Our Ladies" in 1861 and his discharge from the army in 1862, the first period of Thomson's life came to an end. During these twenty-eight years, as I have attempted to show, various influences had worked on him, the general pattern of his thought processes had been established, his temperament had become apparent, and his mature philosophy had been foreshadowed. All these elements are basic to an understanding of Thomson, for they were instrumental in directing the course of his later life and especially in determining the writing he was to do. And all were clearly defined by the time he came to London.

# CHAPTER II

# The Secularist

## 1862-1866

THOMSON came to London immediately after his discharge from the army in October, 1862. There he was welcomed enthusiastically by Charles Bradlaugh, whom he had not seen since his apprentice days, and soon was established in the Bradlaugh home at Tottenham on the north side of London, where he was to remain for four years. Promptly he took his place as a member of the family, which included, in addition to Mr. and Mrs. Bradlaugh, two small girls, Hypatia, four or five years old at the time, and her younger sister, Alice. That Thomson found this life good is not surprising; since he had entered the Royal Caledonian Asylum at the age of eight, the only home he had known was that of the Barneses, where he had stayed during his eighteen months at Ballincollig.

Many details of Thomson's life with the Bradlaughs are to be found in accounts written by Hypatia in later years.[1] Sundays were for the most part devoted to playing with the chil-

---

[1] Hypatia Bradlaugh Bonner, "Childish Recollections of James Thomson," *Our Corner,* August and September, 1886; *Charles Bradlaugh,* I, 109–113.

dren. In the mornings he usually took the two little girls for long walks, and in the afternoons he amused them with extemporaneous fairy tales of brave knights and fair ladies bewitched by fearful hags and befriended by merry brown goblins. When the girls grew older, he told them the stories of the operas, describing the scenes and action in detail and whistling or singing the airs. Later he took them to their first operas and to the Monday Popular Concerts and introduced them to the National Gallery. One wonders if these two little girls were the only companions Thomson had who shared his interest in the arts.

With Bradlaugh he immediately resumed the type of fellowship the two had enjoyed in Ballincollig. Together they spent many long evenings in the small but well-stocked library of the home, smoking till the room was blue and their eyes smarted, talking philosophy, politics, literature, and religion. Hypatia, in terms that point out the contrast between their characters, described the men as they talked: her father sitting bolt upright in a hard straight chair and gesticulating excitedly with his cigar; Thomson leaning back in an easy chair, resting his head on the back, holding the stem of his pipe close to his lips, and saying little.

Mrs. Bradlaugh offered Thomson a somewhat more relaxing companionship, to judge from letters he wrote her in later years.[2] Apparently they chatted pleasantly on happy, trivial, domestic subjects, women's clothes, dances, parties, and even, perhaps, food. The tone of the letters indicates that they en-

---

[2] See especially Thomson's letters to Mrs. Bradlaugh, May 31, 1872, quoted by Salt, *op. cit.*, pp. 78–80; August 7, 1872, quoted pp. 89–90; and September 23, 1872, quoted pp. 91–92.

joyed each other's company and that Mrs. Bradlaugh did not resent Thomson as an intruder in her home.

That Thomson enjoyed this family life is clear. The effect of it on his writing is not, however, equally obvious; yet there are, in my opinion, certain discernible relations. In the first place it was during these years that Thomson produced the so-called "cheerful" poetry, of which "Sunday up the River" is the best known example.[3] In itself this phenomenon would seem of little significance; but when it is noted that he did not again write such poetry until, in the last year of his life, he was once more living in a private home as a member of a family, the probability of a causal relation becomes apparent.[4] A second point is that during these years Thomson's creative abilities were quickest and freest. At no other time did he do so much original work, write so much of high quality, or work with so many forms and types. That he was young, that his health was still reasonably good, and that he was still free from serious financial pressure all undoubtedly contributed; but I think that the companionship of the Bradlaughs and the sense of belonging to a family group also stimulated his creative vitality. This theory gains support from the fact that immediately after he left the Bradlaugh home the amount of poetry he produced began rapidly to decrease. And finally, Thomson did not produce his best works while living in such an environment. Into the writing of "In the Room," "The City of Dreadful Night," and "Insomnia" went the constant, gnawing worry which poverty brought and the depression of spirits attendant on continued ill health; but into them went also,

---

[3] To be considered in detail later in this chapter.
[4] See Chapter V.

and in very large measure, the loneliness of solitude such as he did not know when he was with the Bradlaughs. Had he stayed in that home he would never, I am quite sure, have written those poems.

But more clearly demonstrable than the effects of this life on his work, and at the time much more important, were the results of Thomson's association with the *National Reformer,* a radical, laboring man's weekly, of which Bradlaugh was the editor. As has been noted, a few of Thomson's works had already appeared in print. In February, 1858, "Mr. Save-His-Soul-Alive, O!" a satire in verse, had come out in *The London Investigator,* a journal then published by Bradlaugh. It had been followed late in the year by a prose essay, "Notes on Emerson." Meanwhile "The Fadeless Bower" and "Four Points in a Life," a group of four short lyrics, had appeared in *Tait's Edinburgh Magazine;* and in the next year, 1859, there had been nine more in the same periodical, chief of which were "A Festival of Life," "Tasso to Leonora," "Bertram to the Most Noble and Beautiful Lady Geraldine," and "A Happy Poet." Most of the contributions to *Tait's* had been signed "Crepusculus." In 1859 Thomson had also had two essays in *The Investigator* and had used, for the first time, the signature "B.V.," standing for Bysshe Vanolis, the middle name of Shelley and an anagram made from Novalis. In the following year, 1860, he had four more poems in *Tait's,* and three contributions appeared in the *National Reformer,* of which Bradlaugh had become the editor. A fourth piece had come out in that journal in 1861.[5] It was only natural, therefore, that when Thomson came to London

---

[5] Publication dates are from the bibliography compiled by Bertram Dobell and J. M. Wheeler, in the Mosher edition of *The City of Dreadful Night.*

Bradlaugh encouraged him to write still more for the *National Reformer* and that almost immediately he became a regular contributor.[6]

That Thomson fitted in well with the *National Reformer* is indicated by the fact that for the following thirteen years, until he broke with Bradlaugh in 1875, his work appeared almost exclusively in that journal and that the *National Reformer* printed almost everything he wrote. Obviously, then, an examination of the *National Reformer* will not only tell much about Thomson but also explain many of his works. Such an examination must include a consideration of the Secular Society, for which the *National Reformer* was then the spokesman, and of Charles Bradlaugh, the policy-determining editor, whose personality was reflected in it.

The Secular Society is well characterized by a statement of its purposes from an article titled "Secularism: What It Is," written by Christopher Charles and appearing in the April 18, 1868, and April 25, 1868, issues of the *National Reformer:*

> These ["a few men who have been guided by reason"] reject all the faiths, or such parts of them as do not appear reasonable, hence they have received the names Atheist, Deist, Pantheist, Infidel, Freethinker, Socialist, and, in these modern days, Secularist. . . . Secularism . . . has been applied to that class of conclusions arrived at by

---

[6] Just what Thomson's position on the *National Reformer* was is not clear. In a letter to Dobell, January 18, 1875, quoted by Salt, *op. cit.,* p. 125, he wrote of being on the staff; yet for a number of years he held clerical positions with various other business enterprises. Thus whatever his official position on the *National Reformer* and however he was paid, by salary or by the contribution, it is clear that he did not devote full time to the journal, presumably because he did not receive adequate money from it to live on.

reason, derived from the observation and experience of mankind. . . . Secularism . . . is a name under which is taught the duty man has to perform today, the work of the present age. Its principles concern men in this world, the truth of which can be tested in this life. It takes reason for its guide, morality for its principle, and utility as the test of all the actions and institutions of men. . . . Secularism adopts reason instead of faith, science instead of revelation, nature instead of providence, work instead of worship and prayer, and holds that humanity, instead of divinity, should occupy the thought of men and command their service. . . . Nature interpreted by science presents order and method, by the study of which man obtains a guide for daily life—obedience to the laws of conditions of existence being the only mode of living a useful and healthy life. . . . All who comply with the invariable laws of phenomena reap the same results. . . . The final test of actions and institutions is, do they tend to human improvement, and the increase of human happiness? [7]

To the Secular Society belonged not only the Bradlaughs but almost everyone else with whom Thomson had contact during these years and, in fact, in his later years. And it was the Secularist Burial Service, written by the close friend of the latter part of his life, Austin Holyoake, which was read over his grave by Theodore Wright, another close Secularist friend.

---

[7] Thomson himself in his *Address on the Opening of the New Hall of the Leicester Secular Society*, March 6, 1881, also characterized Secularism, but less fully. A more complete concept of the nature of Secularism may be gained from the many articles on the subject and from the question and answer department of the *National Reformer*. See also Gilmour, *Champion of Liberty: Charles Bradlaugh*, pp. 79-80.

For many years Bradlaugh was the most widely known of the Secularists, partly because he was editor of the *National Reformer* and partly because of his character. A proselyting atheist and social reformer, he either talked into submission or outshouted those who dared meet him in debate; and his lectures were noted for their heavily sarcastic personal remarks. Crude, coarse, and boisterous, he delighted in any kind of publicity for himself and his cause: boastfully he related stories of fist fights in which he bested four or five opponents at a time, and he welcomed triumphantly arrest and a night or two in a vermin-infested jail. (In justice, it must be admitted that he was often held illegally.) Lacking Thomson's imaginative sympathy, he was stubbornly intolerant; his attitude towards Christians was no less bigoted than theirs towards him. But in spite of these unattractive characteristics he commanded great respect for his remarkable energy, sincerity, and physical and moral courage. He believed in his ideal and worked honestly and to the limit of his endurance for it.[8]

That the *National Reformer* reflected the ideals of both the Secular Society and of Bradlaugh is seen in the statement of policy, which also indicates the nature and subject matter of the most of its copy:

> Editorially the *National Reformer,* as to religious questions is, and always has been, as far as we are concerned, the advocate of Atheism; it teaches that all the religions of the world are based on error; that humanity is higher than theology; that knowledge is far preferable to faith; that action is more effective than prayer; and that the best worship man can offer is honest work, in order to

---

[8] Bonner, *Charles Bradlaugh;* Gilmour, *op. cit.*

make one another wiser and happier than heretofore. In politics, we are Radicals of a very extreme kind; we are advocates of manhood sufferage; we desire shorter Parliaments; laws which will be more equal in their application to master and servant; protection from the present state of the laws which make pheasants more valuable than peasants; we desire the repeal of the laws against blasphemy, and the enactment of some measure which will make all persons competent as witnesses whatever their opinions on religion; we advocate the separation of Church and State, and join with the financial reformers in their efforts to reduce our enormous and extravagant national expenditures.[9]

The sensational methods employed in its make-up give further evidence of its character. The issue of April 12, 1868, carrying a black-bordered box in the middle of the front page, was typical:

> MURDERED
> at Montigny, ten Laborers
> and one Laborer's Wife, by
> the troops and gendarmerie
> representing the right of
> Capital to reduce Wages.

Such was the publication for which Thomson wrote for thirteen years.[10]

---

[9] Reiteration of policies by Bradlaugh, in *National Reformer,* February, 1862.

[10] The characterization of this journal is based on my examination of the John Crerar Library file of the *National Reformer,* the only one in the United States nearly complete.

Naturally there were disadvantages attendant on his close association with this type of paper. His chances for literary reputation while working for the journal were, if not completely nullified, at least reduced to a minimum, for no one known as a regular writer for the *National Reformer* could expect an unprejudiced hearing from either the critics or the public at large.[11] On the other hand there were advantages. Because his own religious and political convictions coincided in general with those of the *National Reformer*, Thomson was not forced to tailor his ideas to sell his work; he was free to write as he wished. That he was fully conscious and appreciative of this advantage he noted in a passage in "Bumble, Bumbledom, and Bumbleism": "Luckily I am an author thoroughly unknown, and writing for a periodical of deepest disrepute. One is very free, with no name to lose; and one is freer still, with such a name that it cannot possibly be lost for a worse; and between us [himself and the *National Reformer*] we possess both these happy freedoms."

Much of the writing Thomson did during this period showed no influence whatsoever of the *National Reformer;* on the other hand, much showed clearly its mark. Of this latter group the best are the satires, which fall into two classes, the nonreligious and the religious. There are but two major examples of the nonreligious satire: the rather dull, overly long "Bumble, Bumbledom, and Bumbleism," 1865, a charge that Englishmen were not only impervious to new ideas but were actually so afraid of them that they set up machines to combat them, chief of which was the press; and the gay, amusing

---

[11] Salt, *op. cit.,* p. 54. Thomson himself commented in a diary entry of March 21, 1880, that working for the *National Reformer* was "anything but a recommendation."

"Liberty and Necessity," 1866, a gibe at the Secularists, who preached necessitarianism but assumed liberty in their own actions. Of the religious satires, however, there are more examples. Prior to his coming to London, Thomson had indicated an interest in religious satire in his first published poem, "Mr. Save-His-Soul-Alive, O!" a slight bit of verse showing more promise in concept than in execution. This interest naturally received stimulation and encouragement in the offices of the *National Reformer,* and the first of Thomson's writings to be published in that journal following his arrival in London was the religious satire, "The Established Church." This was followed in 1865 and 1866 by six more.[12]

All seven of these satires are similar in character. Typical is "Mr. Kingsley's Convertites," which pointed out that Kingsley's heroes were heathens when healthy and happy and turned Christian only when ill or unfortunate. But of the seven, "Christmas Eve in the Upper Circles" is the best; indeed it is, in my opinion, the best of any of his satires.[13] "Christmas Eve" was written with much care (and obviously with much enjoyment), and although the concept is not subtle, the method frequently is. There are quick allusions, as to Addison, who is

---

[12] "The Story of a Famous Old Firm," 1865; "One Thing Needful," 1865; "Mr. Kingsley's Convertites," 1865; "The Athanasian Creed," 1866; "Jesus: as God; as Man," 1866; and "Christmas Eve in the Upper Circles," 1866.

[13] G. W. Foote, in his "Preface," *Satires and Profanities,* wrote, "The late Professor Clifford considered *The Story of a Famous Old Jewish Firm* a piece of exquisite mordant satire worthy of Swift." Salt, however, speaks more moderately of Thomson's "relationship with Swift" (*op. cit.,* p. 328). He remarks that one of Thomson's later satires, "Proposals for the Speedy Extinction of Evil and Misery," reminds one of Swift. I can agree with Salt only if his comment is restricted to the title. In "Christmas Eve," which I believe is the best of Thomson's satires, I see no influence of Swift or of any other satirist in particular.

still in hell because he "hasn't got quit for his death-bed brandy yet." There are brief, suggestive comparisons, as when God admits his envy of Zeus, "for a joyous life the rogue led," and continues, "So I, like an old fool, must have my amour; and a pretty intrigue I got into with the prim damsel Mary!" There are ludicrous elements, as the racial troubles between the black and white angels in heaven. There is a playing with words, as in the phrase in which God describes the saints, "The whimpering, simpering, canting chanting blockheads!" In the tale God, tired of being overruled by his pasty-faced and anemic son, "looking sublimely good and respectable," rebels. First, he refuses flatly to take part in the Christmas festivities in Heaven; then he calls up Swift and Sterne from the lower regions, where Christ had consigned them so that his father might not suffer from their evil influences, to join him and Rabelais, for whom he has already sent. Demanding something better than the Lachrymae Christi on which he has been choking, he shuts himself up with his disreputable cronies for a two weeks' drinking bout, by the end of which time Christmas will be well over.

Sharply contrasting with the irreligious tone of the satires, well shown in "Christmas Eve," is another less obvious but more important element, an undercurrent of profound esteem, almost love, for Christ as a man and for true Christians. Because this attitude is expressed in the satires only in flashes, chiefly in single sentences which suddenly shift from the general tone of ridicule to one of respect, one finds the best definition of it not in them but in "Open Secret Societies," written in the same year as three of the satires, 1865, but unlike them showing almost no influence of the *National Reformer*. In section ii of the essay, after having condemned various organizations and institutions which had taken the names of the saints,

[ 49 ]

Thomson with a quick change of mood apologized to the true saints:

> Belovèd and pure and beautiful souls, these whom I was mocking are not of you, though indeed they assume your name; they are of the fraternities of those who in your lifetimes mocked and hated and persecuted and killed you; they have caught up your solemn passwords because these are now passwords to wealth and worldly honour, which for you were passwords to the prison and the scaffold and the stake; they have clothed themselves with your sheep's clothing because wolves have long been extinct in our England, and sheep browse securely in the fattest pastures by the sweetest rivers; but they hate with a bitter hatred and fear all who are possessed by the spirit which possessed you; . . . they desecrate your holy mysteries, they stereotype your rapturous prayers into jargon and cant; for your eucharistic wine they have publican's gin-and-water, and your eucharistic bread they butter on both sides and flavour with slander at tea. Even I, poor heathen and cynic, am nearer to you, ye holy ones, than are ninety-nine in a hundred of these.

This respect for the sincere was characteristic of Thomson. In writing of Shelley's belief in the perfectibility of man, for example, he commented, "Though I must consider Shelley mistaken in this belief, I yet honour and not blame him for it. For his nature must have been most pure and noble, since it could persuade his peculiarly introspective mind of its truth." [14] And in writing of Browning's Christianity, he remarked, ". . . but candid Non-Christians (among whom I am fain to be classed) cannot but recognize and esteem the fearless and

---

[14] "Shelley," 1860.

fervent Christianity of those poems, cannot but thoroughly admit the great poet's burning sincerity. . . ." [15]

It is not, however, insincerity that was Thomson's main point of attack in the satires. Rather he assailed, with but few exceptions, the logic, the thought processes of an individual, an organization, an institution, pointing out inconsistencies, contradictions, and fallacies. Such analytic treatment forms the basis of most of the essays and is, therefore, difficult to illustrate briefly, but a short passage from "A Word on Blasphemy" shows the method applied to a small point: [16]

> The most Christian S. R. [*Saturday Review*] says to the Atheist Iconoclast [Bradlaugh], You blaspheme. Whom? The Christian God! And the S. R. does not appear to see that it is assuming the very existence of God which is in dispute between itself and Iconoclast. For the Atheist, God is a figment, nothing; in blaspheming God he therefore blasphemes nothing.

Despite this intellectual, analytic approach, typical of Thomson in all his work and thinking, the humor of most of the satires is genial and good-natured, as is shown in "Christmas Eve." None of his religious satires and very few of his non-religious ones are marked by bitterness or even intensity of feeling. Nor were they motivated by high moral purpose; Thomson's audience already agreed with him, so he wrote far

---

[15] "Notes on the Genius of Robert Browning," 1882.

[16] "A Word on Blasphemy" is actually a selection from a long article, "*The Saturday Review* and the *National Reformer*," thus titled by the editor, G. W. Foote, for inclusion in *Satires and Profanities*. The original article appeared in the *National Reformer*, April 28, 1867, and May 5, 1867. It does not properly, therefore, belong in this chapter, but the illustration it affords is briefer than any offered by essays of the period under consideration and is typical.

more to amuse than to persuade. Thus the quality of their humor is usually amiable rather than caustic.

In addition to the satires, which show the influence of the *National Reformer*, there are equally important essays which, as I have earlier indicated, do not show such influence. These do not, however, fall into any single, well-defined category; the subjects and the methods of treating them are as many as there are essays. Moreover the importance of each is best gauged and its significance made clearest when considered in relation to other works. I choose, therefore, only to list them at this point, leaving consideration of them until a more appropriate time. "The Poems of William Blake," 1864, will be discussed in Chapter IV with other essays in criticism. "Per Contra: The Poet, High Art, Genius," 1865, and "A Lady of Sorrow," 1862–1864, more properly described as a phantasy than an essay, will both be taken up later in this chapter. Already mentioned and to be touched on from time to time in the following pages is "Open Secret Societies," 1865. These four are Thomson's major personal essays of the period.

Very different in character from the nonfiction prose are Thomson's narratives.[17] It must be conceded at the outset

---

[17] In treating Thomson's three pieces of fiction as all belonging to this period I am being somewhat arbitrary, for only one is dated, "Seen Thrice: A London Study," written in 1863. This was first printed in *The Secularist*, July 8, 1876, and July 15, 1876, and later reprinted in the March and April issues of *Progress*, 1885.

The second narrative, "Sarpolus of Mardon," which appeared in the February, March, April, May, and June issues of *Progress*, 1887, bore no date of composition; but Dobell included "The Siren's Song," very probably from the work, with Thomson's "early" poems, a group which includes works as late as 1864, in vol. II of *The Poetical Works*. He added the note, "This lyric forms a portion of a romantic story called *Sarpolus of Mardon*. . . ." The lyric, however, does not appear in the version of the narrative printed in *Progress*, though the editor com-

that these are of inferior quality; yet they demand more consideration than their merits alone would warrant because, so far as I know, the fact that Thomson attempted fiction has never been discussed. Salt did not mention it. Indeed, the Leopardi fragment is not listed as such even in the Dobell bibliography.

The first of the three tales, "Seen Thrice: A London Study," is a sketch which implies rather than tells a story by means of three high lights in a life. But in spite of the quiet, restrained manner, the brevity with which Thomson treats the theatrical scenes, and several excellent descriptive passages, the story is forced and unnatural, chiefly because the threefold device makes for a melodramatic effect which overshadows the realistic qualities meant to sound a note of tragedy. The tale is further weakened by its strained ending.

Of Thomson's second story, "Sarpolus of Mardon," even

---

mented on a reference made in the text to such a song: "The song does not appear in the author's ms., and perhaps it was never written." The lyric Dobell printed fits the tale very well, and there is no reasonable doubt that he and the editor of *Progress* were speaking of the same song. Dobell, who knew Thomson's work better than anyone else, probably had good grounds for dating the poem as "early." An early date is further indicated by the fact that the imagery of "Sarpolus of Mardon" is very similar to that of "A Festival of Life," 1857, and Part II of "A Lady of Sorrow," 1862–1864.

The third piece of fiction appeared in the June 14, 1891, issue of the *National Reformer,* headed by a note: "The following uncompleted and unnamed story was, apparently, written at one sitting. It is undated, but as the manuscript is penned on the backs of unfilled certificate forms of the Royal Alhambra Palace Company, Limited, dated 186–, presumably the fragment was written about 1870. . . ." Such dating, however, assumes (a) that Thomson came into possession of or used the forms only after the turn of the decade made them obsolete, (b) that the company was operative throughout the entire decade. It seems to me equally reasonable that this piece was written in the same general period as the dated "Seen Thrice" and the probably early "Sarpolus."

less may be said in commendation. The narrative reads like a cross between a fairy story with a helpful dwarf and an Oriental tale with scenes of great court splendor. It is too artificial to arouse the reader's sympathy and too elaborate and detailed to hold his interest. The Oriental names are so strange and numerous that he becomes confused; and to make his confusion complete, there are many references, which add still more names, to events which took place before the story opens.[18] The descriptions, especially that of the underground vault which is the burial place of Sarpolus' ancestors, are vivid; but like the descriptions in Beckford's *Vathek*, to which they are very similar, they interrupt a story that moves too slowly at best. It is possible that Thomson recognized these faults for, after having got well into the narrative, he dropped it and never made any effort to complete it.

The third story, unnamed and, like "Sarpolus of Mardon," unfinished, tells of a pianist, Leopardi, who, by means of his remarkable (perhaps supernatural) musical abilities throws his listeners into a trance. But despite the fact that the twenty-five hundred words were clearly meant to be the introduction to a story, there is no hint whatsoever how one might evolve from the situation. Moreover, the tone is so intense that it is almost impossible to conceive of a complete narrative sustained at such a high pitch. I am of the opinion that Thomson probably had no plot in mind, that this fragment was rather the expression of his emotional reaction to some music which had especially moved him.

It is impossible, I think, to find any close association

---

[18] The name of one character is not Oriental: Vanolis. An examination of the story shows, however, no relationship between the character and Thomson.

between the first two narrative attempts and Thomson's life or other works, although it is true that the method employed in "Seen Thrice" was probably suggested by his reading of Browning and that the Orientalism of "Sarpolus" calls to mind other examples of at least a fleeting interest in the East: his explanatory note to "The Doom," that the City of Statues was from the *Arabian Nights;* his later poem, "Weddah and Om-el-Bonain," based on an Oriental theme; and his translations of parts of Goethe's "Westöstlicher Divan."

But the relation of the Leopardi piece to his life is clear. From the time that he came to London till his death music was, as I have noted, one of his chief sources of pleasure. Before going to the opera, he studied the text carefully that his enjoyment might be more complete.[19] At the Monday Popular Concerts in St. James's Hall, which he attended as regularly as his finances permitted, he pored over the miniature scores, following closely the development of the music— first subject, second subject, working out, free phantasia, recapitulation. In addition to learning the various forms and how to follow them, he acquainted himself with the best composers, their works, and their characteristics. The Beethoven quartets especially pleased him; Schubert, Schumann, and Mendelssohn he found too romantic, melifluous, and undisciplined.[20] That he should attempt to convey, as he did in the Leopardi piece, the emotional trance into which music may draw one gives evidence of his own reactions to music.

But why did Thomson attempt fiction at all? There are several possible answers. This was the period of his life at

---

[19] P. B. Marston's obituary notice of Thomson, *Athenaeum,* June 10, 1882.

[20] Thomson, "Jottings," *National Reformer,* November 15, 1874.

which his creative vitality seems to have been highest; it may
have been that he attempted fiction simply as an experiment,
to see if he could do it. Or it may have been that, in his
desire to place his work with more reputable periodicals, he
was trying a form from which he could most easily divorce
his own thoughts and feelings and thereby avoid offending
the conservatism of a respectable editor. Or he may have
been trying to write mere potboilers, acceptable to any journal
which paid more than the *National Reformer*.

But if the reason that Thomson attempted fiction is open
to question, the major cause of his failure is sure. And it is
this point which emphasizes one aspect of his mind, nowhere
more clearly defined: the characters of his fiction fail to live.
The same is true of the characters of Thomson's three narrative poems, "Ronald and Helen," written during his army
period, and "Two Lovers" and "Weddah and Om-el-Bonain,"
written later; in all, the characters are mere puppets who move
mechanically on the strings of the narrative, although the failure in the poems is less obvious because of the music and
rhythm. Throughout Thomson's work it is apparent that he
was interested chiefly in ideas and that his creative ability lay
primarily in their expression. Although the record of his personal life shows that he liked people individually, and although
his work, even "The City of Dreadful Night," a poem of
ideas, proves that his sympathy for the human race was deep
and broad, human beings as individuals were not grist for the
mill of his mind. Further proof that Thomson's interest lay
in ideas rather than in characters will be noted in Chapter IV,
wherein I will consider his literary criticism. There it will be
observed that his judgment of authors was based on their

ideas and their method of handling ideas, not on their skill with characters or plot.

Far more creditable than his narratives were his translations from German, French, and Italian literature. His success in this field was the result, I believe, of three things: his knowledge of the languages was thorough and in the case of Italian, at least, included an interest in roots and derivations; he translated only that which he wished to read for his own pleasure; and finally, he had a positive and well-defined theory of translation.

That theory he stated in a long note attached to his version of Novalis' "Hymns to Night," dated "Thursday, 7/5/'66." [21] A translator should choose only short poems, since they alone can be effectively translated. Moreover he should not attempt all the poems in a collection but only those which "favour him beforehand with glimpses of a happy version. . . . Success in translating a short poem often depends upon catching a felicitous version of some one line which is the key-note or dominant phrase of the whole. . . ." Once a poem had been

---

[21] This note is found in a notebook in the possession of Mr. Percy Dobell (who graciously made it available to me) which contains a number of poems and translations by Thomson, along with a few press notices (and remarks on them by Bertram Dobell) and poems written in memory of Thomson. The poems and translations are all copied from Thomson's manuscripts and are entirely authentic. Dobell appended to the small volume a prefatory note, explaining its contents: "Note:—The poems contained in this volume are by James Thomson ('B.V.'). They are nearly all unpublished, not having been included in the collected edition of his works (1895). They are for the most part of inferior merit, and were excluded by me on that account. This does not apply, of course, to the translations of Novalis, which should be published, I think, someday, though with a note stating that the translation never received the author's final revision."

selected on these bases, it was the responsibility of the translator to determine whether it could be better done freely or literally. In the matter of stanzaic division and meter, however, the translator had no such license; "with very rare exceptions" these were to be strictly followed. Paraphrasing or "dilution of the original" he condemned as "sacred to noodles." In addition to these dicta Thomson expressed a more general idea concerning translations: that if translators were not forced by their jealousy and selfishness to make their version of a piece entirely and wholly their own, really excellent translations might be arrived at by combining the best of several translators. "From the well-chosen attempts of various translators, a really valuable anthology might be collected by a gardener who did not fear to engraft and prune and transplant."

The chief excellence of this theory, and the resultant excellence of Thomson's own translations, lies in the loyalty to the author being translated. If one attempts only those works which have favored him with glimpses of a happy version, he brings to his task enthusiasm and freshness and feeling for the work; if he attempts the whole, he is unfair to the author, for some of the work will be drudgery, and the retention of the spirit of the original will be impossible. That loyalty to the author is further indicated by Thomson's suggestion that better translations would result if translators would surrender the prerogatives of their own individuality and permit compilations. Throughout Thomson emphasizes the importance of the author and the original and ignores the translator save as an instrument.

Thomson's first translations of Heine's poems were made, as has been noted, when he was in the army. From that time on he turned out a few each year until 1866. The total number I judge to be about fifty, some printed in various journals during his life, some not printed until after his death, some never printed at all, about twenty-five collected in Volume I of the *Poetical Works*.[22] For the most part they are successful; both versions of "The Greek Gods," "The Pilgrimage to Kelvaar," and the short sentimental love poems all have the flavor of the original. On the other hand some are too literal; although Thomson was pleased with his version of "Die Lorelei," it seems to me heavy, almost pedestrian. Best are those with a satirical turn, such as "Reminiscence of Harmonia" and "In Harbour." The daughter of Karl Marx thought so highly of those she saw that she copied them and sent them to her father,[23] who enthusiastically wrote Thomson that they were "no translation, but a reproduction of the original, such as Heine himself, if master of the English language would have given." [24] George Saintsbury, less effusive but still commendatory, wrote that the songs were as good "as any we have seen."

The unpublished translation of Novalis' "Hymns to Night," available only in the above-mentioned notebook,[25] is both complete and accurate. The artificiality of language, the straining for effect, and the cloying, melancholy sentimentalism of the original are noticeable especially in the prose passages; the poetry, like that of the original, is somewhat simpler. In accordance with his theory of translation, Thomson kept closely to the original; he followed the proportions of prose and poetry and retained the stanzaic divisions,

---

[22] The notebook contains eighteen pages of Heine translations, almost all love poems, none of which were printed in the *Poetical Works*.

[23] Diary, June 15, 1880.

[24] Quoted by Salt, *op. cit.*, p. 263.

[25] See footnote 21, p. 57.

the meter, and even the rhyme scheme. The following parallel passages of the poetry from section iv show the strictness with which he kept to Novalis, though this is the one passage of the whole in which he permitted himself the liberty of changing the form, combining two dimeters into one tetrameter:

| | |
|---|---|
| Hinüber wall ich, | I journey onwards and every brier |
| Und jede Pein | |
| Wird einst ein Stachel | Is but a spur to my swift desire. |
| Der Wollust sein. | |
| Noch wenig Zeiten, | A short time now, and free I rest, |
| So bin ich los | |
| Und liege trunken | And lie bliss-drunken in Love's |
| Der Lieb im Schoss. | own breast. |
| Unendliches Leben | The life immortal swells mighty |
| Wogt mächtig in mir, | in me; |
| Ich schaue von oben | From the realm I look down to |
| Herunter nach dir. | thee. |
| An jenem Hügel | On yonder hillock is quenched |
| Verlischt dein Glanz— | thy shine, |
| Ein Schatten bringet | A shadow bringeth the crown |
| Den kühlenden Kranz. | divine. |
| O! sauge, Geliebter, | O draw me beloved, draw me |
| Gewaltig mich an, | above, |
| Dass ich entschlummern | That I may die into very Love. |
| Und lieben kann. | |
| Ich fühle des Todes | I fear Death's youth-renewing |
| Verjüngende Flut, | flood, |
| Zu Balsam und Äther | To balsam and ether transform |
| Verwandelt mein Blut— | my blood. |
| Ich lebe bei Tage | I live by day all hope and faith |
| Voll Glauben und Mut | |
| Und sterbe die Nächte | And nightly die into holy death. |
| In heiliger Glut. | |

That he did not revise the work for publication is due, I believe, to his discovery that he was no longer, if indeed he ever had been, in sympathy with Novalis. When Matilda died, he had, imagining a romantic kinship with the German, adopted an anagram of Novalis as part of his pseudonym, probably without ever having read any of his works. Later, still imagining the kinship, he set himself to translating the "Hymns," which Novalis had written in sorrow for his dead sweetheart. Once at the task, however, Thomson likely realized that in spirit he and the German had nothing in common; the "Hymns," which start as songs in praise of a vague concept in which night, love, and death are more or less identified and shift less than halfway through into a paean of Christianity, could have had no appeal for him apart from their sentimental interest. On the contrary, their mysticism must have almost repelled him. Accordingly, the preliminary translation complete, Thomson dropped all work on the project. Heine was more to his taste.

During this period Thomson also translated one piece of German prose, Goethe's "Israel in the Wilderness," to which he attached the comment that German prose is "a lumbering vehicle for the conveyance of thought—even when horsed and driven by such a master as Goethe." [26] And he made his only translations from the French, two poems of Béranger, "The Good God" and "The Death of the Devil." [27] The latter is, in my opinion, one of the most successful attempts,

---

[26] In the essay, "The Divan of Goethe," printed in 1871, are included several passages translated from the "Westöstlicher Divan," totaling some 110 lines, along with a passage from Heine's "De l'Allemagne" on the "Divan." The only other translation from Goethe that I have been able to find is "Prometheus," undated.

[27] Included in Thomson's later essay on Flaubert's *Temptation of St. Anthony* are translations of several passages. There are, however, no translations of entire works.

probably because the idea appealed to him and the tone, one of good-humored irony, was congenial. His most important translations, those of the Leopardi essays and dialogues, belong to a later period.

The best known of Thomson's works of this period are his Cockney poems, "Sunday up the River," "Sunday at Hampstead," "Polycrates," "Shameless," "Low Life," and "Aquatics," all written in 1865.[28] These poems, differing from both his earlier and later verse,[29] show certain common characteristics. The first of these is the subject matter, doubtless suggested by Thomson's associates at the time. At the Secular Society parties his fellow guests were members of the working class, clerks, shopkeepers' assistants, underground guards, seamstresses, charwomen, provisioners. In "Vane's Story" he described such a party and the people who attended it:

> The mere tame weekly gathering
> Of humble tradesmen, lively clerks,
> And fair ones who befit such sparks:
> Few merry meetings could look duller;
> No wealth, no grandeur, no rich colour.
> Yet they enjoy it: give a girl
> Some fiddle-screech to time her whirl,
> And give a youth the limpest waist
> That wears a gown to hold embraced.

---

[28] Taking the term Cockney poetry from "An Idyll of Cockaigne," the subtitle to "Sunday up the River," I have substituted it for the phrase commonly used by the critics, "cheerful poetry," which seems to me to place undue emphasis on a quality of little significance. I use it to cover all those poems similar in subject matter, treatment, and tone.

[29] There is an exception to this statement. In the last six months of Thomson's life, he wrote "Richard Forest's Midsummer Night," "At Belvoir," "A Modern Penelope," and "The Sleeper," all of which show a resemblance to the Cockney poetry. For a discussion of these poems, see Chapter V.

These are the figures that move through the Cockney poetry, and their activities are its subject.

In all these poems Thomson's approach was impersonal and objective; he wrote of what he saw, not of what he felt or thought. This deviation from his usual attitude he pointed out in a chance but significant remark. When told of a criticism of the colors he had used in describing the costume of a rower in "Sunday up the River," he answered "with a slight sneer," "Do they think *I* ever went rowing in that style? I write what I have seen." [30] Whether his readers liked the characters was a matter of indifference to Thomson; his purpose was to give a photographic picture.

Throughout these poems the tone is the same; to any might be attached the subtitle of "Sunday at Hampstead," "An idle idyll by a very humble member of the great and noble London mob." And the tone is set by the action: the events, usually of a holiday or some part of it, in the life of a pair of young lovers of the working class. A fair sample of the group is "Sunday up the River"—more than fair, perhaps, since it contains a few fine lyrics and a few felicitous descriptions.

Ever since their first appearance critics have, in my opinion, consistently overvalued these poems and in their enthusiasm they have ignored two serious faults. In the first place, because the detail is usually photographic rather than significant, as in the case of the "mauve purple shaded" cravat and the red wool shirt to which objection was made, it distracts the reader. And in the second place, the poems are not raised above the commonplace by any depth of emotion or any meaning beyond the surface one. Only in "Low Life," the most successful of the group, did Thomson go below the surface. In it, by means

---

[30] Quoted by G. W. Foote, "James Thomson. II. The Poet," *Progress,* June, 1884.

of a short episode, he suggested that man is by nature so egocentric that his sympathies are at best weak, shallow, and short-lived.

In seeking for an explanation of these faults, which are not characteristic of Thomson's other works, I come to an aspect of the poems which has never been pointed out, their reflection of Thomson's attitude towards his own life at the time they were written. This attitude is made clear by more than a half-dozen works but especially in the essay "Per Contra: The Poet, High Art, Genius," 1865.[31] The essay makes two major points. First, the finest expression of life must be immediate; it is perfect in proportion to its spontaneity. No art is immediate; since it is always mediate, it can never be completely spontaneous. Therefore, art is not the best, the perfect form of expression; the perfect forms are such immediate and spontaneous reactions as laughter, dancing, tears, impulsive physical action. The second of the two points is that "artistry accuses weakness and lack of vitality in the artist." The artist is an artist because he has neither the strength nor the virility to participate actively in life; he stands aloof, not because of circumstances or personal inclination but because a lack in his own nature forces him to do so.

> He sings of that which he cannot enjoy, cannot achieve;
> if at any time he can enjoy, can achieve, be sure he is
> not then pondering or singing it. Where and when rich
> life is present, it lives, and does not content itself with

---

[31] "A Lady of Sorrow," 1862–1864, "The Fire That Filled My Heart of Old," 1864, "Open Secret Societies," 1865, "Sayings of Sigvat," 1865, "Art," 1865, "Philosophy," 1866, "Life's Hebe," 1866, and "The Naked Goddess," 1866–1867.

shadowing forth and celebrating life. When and where rich life is not present, the shadowing forth and celebration of life may partially console for its absence, or may even partially illude into the belief in its presence. Yet life remains and ever is superior to art as a man to the picture of a man.[32]

Clearly Thomson felt, as he had earlier when he wrote the verses on his twenty-third birthday, that he could not enjoy, could not achieve, that his life was not rich, that it lacked emotional vitality. And this attitude is reflected in and explains the Cockney poems, explains Thomson's emotionless, objective approach to them. He was writing merely of what he had seen.

Entirely different from the impersonal Cockney poems are the two frankly personal works, "Vane's Story," 1864, and "A Lady of Sorrow," 1862–1864. These, the most significant works of this period, are closely associated with "The Doom of a City" and "To Our Ladies of Death," both written before Thomson came to London.[33] In the earlier poems Thomson had expressed for the first time certain of the ideas which were to become parts of his mature philosophy; [34] in these later works he stated the same ideas with more sureness and added to them. "The City of Dreadful Night" is, of course, the culmination of all four; in fact it might be said that they are but a series of studies leading to that great poem.

---

[32] "Per Contra."

[33] Thomson pointed out in notes to both "Our Ladies" and "A Lady" the relation of the works to De Quincey's "Suspiria de Profundis." But more than mutual inspiration or even closeness of ideas is indicated by the similarity of the titles. The earlier, "To Our Ladies," 1861, is actually a poetic study for the later prose piece.

[34] See Chapter I.

Neither "Vane's Story," in verse, nor "A Lady," in prose, is of high literary quality; both show many faults, most serious of which is their structural weakness. This fault is especially obvious in "Vane's Story," a long, episodic piece which fails almost completely to give any sense of unity; the episodes, each treated in a different style, no two of comparable weight, have little in common save the characters, and these are not so handled as to weld the parts into an organic whole.

Of these episodes, that which has engaged the most attention from Matilda-enamored critics is the one wherein Vane (Thomson) likens his life to a fountain hitherto stopped up by dead leaves and stones but now released by an unnamed vision, obviously Matilda. Much more revealing than this romantic allegory, however, is an earlier episode in which Vane and Matilda converse, Matilda questioning and accusing and Vane answering and explaining.[35] In Vane's responses, of course, are the principal autobiographical material and the deepest emotion.

The depth of emotion is expressed by means of a contrast between form and feeling. The use of commonplace, often colloquial, diction, of a half-bantering tone established partially

---

[35] Although there is no external evidence that Thomson read Goethe's *Faust* in either the original or translation, it is echoed in so many places in this section that one is impelled to believe that he was well acquainted with it. The whole situation of Margaret's questioning Faust on his religion in "Martha's Garden" is close to that of Matilda's questioning Vane. An idea expressed in the "Witch's Kitchen,"

Damned to old hornbooks, and the Gothic letter:
Though for all that mankind don't seem much better,

is repeated, though in an expanded form, even to some of its phraseology. And the apparently flippant cynicism veiling sincere thoughts and emotion, characteristic of many of Mephistopheles' speeches, especially in the "Prologue in Heaven," is characteristic also of Vane's responses to Matilda.

by the diction and partially by light touches of mocking exaggeration, and of undignified couplets and short lines of only
three or four feet to convey thoughts on subjects traditionally
treated with polysyllabic solemnity gives a first impression
of flippant, almost cheap, cynicism. Yet underneath the apparent shallowness there runs a current of sincerity and honesty
that is frequently harsh because it is somewhat defensive and
somewhat belligerent. This contrast between the effect of
superficiality created by the form and the underlying feeling
lends a particular emotional force to this episode of the poem.
Both the means by which Thomson achieved this effect and
the emotion itself are to be seen in following quotations.

The major idea in this episode is that the laws of the universe
are immutable and unconscious of human existence. In "The
Doom of a City" Thomson had presented one aspect of this
concept in his consideration of the indifference of nature to
man, but he had shown his reluctance to accept it by insisting
at the same time on the idea of a divine plan. Now, seven years
later, he expresses the full concept without reservations and
emphasizes its deterministic implications. Of these the most
important is that in a universe so governed man is not only not
perfectible but not even capable of improvement through his
own efforts. By way of evidence Thomson cites Shelley,
Socrates, Joan of Arc, Swift, Luther, and many other meliorists:

> In these, and in how many more,
> Have I outbattled life's stern war,
> Endured all hardships, toiled and fought,
> Oppressed, sore-wounded, and distraught,
> While inwardly consumed with thought;
> How long! how long!—Mankind no whit
> The better for the whole of it!

A second implication Thomson does not develop at length nor, indeed, even state explicitly. Rather he hints it in a passage whose surface theme, that of sympathy for man, is underlined by the suggestion that men, being helpless to change themselves or their lives in the face of immutable laws, are not morally responsible for what they are or what they do.[36]

> "Now my gross, earthly, human heart
> With man and not with God takes part;
> With men, however vile, and not
> With seraphim I cast my lot:
> With those poor ruffian thieves, too strong
> To starve amidst our social wrong,
> And yet too weak to wait and earn
> Dry bread by honest labour stern;
> With those poor harlots steeping sin
> And shame and woe in vitriol-gin:
> Shall these, so hardly dealt with here,
> Be worse off in a future sphere;
> And I, a well-fed lounger, seek
> To 'cut' them dead, to cringe and sneak
> Into that bland *beau monde* the sky,
> Whose upper circles are so high?"

It is also in this episode that Thomson, reviewing his earlier years, explained his "sin" as his religious doubts and disbelief and implied that his moods of frantic remorse born of that "sin" were over.[37]

The second of the autobiographical works of this period, "A Lady of Sorrow," offers even more material than "Vane's

---

[36] This idea he had expressed more fully and positively in an earlier essay, "Liberty and Necessity," 1866.

[37] See Chapter I.

Story." This prose phantasy starts out as the story of Thomson's grief at the death of Matilda. He is visited first by the Angel, who comforts him with the hope of reunion after death; but soon she becomes the Siren, symbol of futile rebellion, born of reckless, passionately bitter despair. Shortly, the Siren is replaced by the Shadow, who promises oblivious death. The first two sections, dealing with the Angel and the Siren, are both very short, together making up but one-fifth of the whole, and are of comparatively little interest. The third part, that of the Shadow, however, is worthy of detailed consideration.

The mood of this section, one of weariness of spirit and a longing for the repose of death, is apparent throughout; but its most striking expression is in the litany of death, chanted by the Shadow. This litany, made up of twenty-eight quotations from Plato, the Bible, Chaucer, Shakespeare, Keats, Arnold, and others, all voicing the same deep desire for the peace of death, has a cumulative effect of emotional lassitude, almost exhaustion. One cannot state categorically that such was the predominant mood of Thomson during these years; in fact, an examination of all his writings would seem unquestionably to refute any such assumption. Yet that he had at hand such a collection of quotations on the subject of the peace of death and that the mood permeated a work which he took two years to write bears evidence that this weariness and desire for release was more than a thing of the moment.

It is in this section also that Thomson expressed most directly the philosophic ideas with which he was chiefly concerned during these years. These ideas fall into two groups, one reflecting the earlier stages in the development of his thought and the other looking forward to his final philosophy.

The first group includes two ideas which Thomson had considered, the one only casually, the other seriously, in his efforts to find a substitute for orthodox Christianity. The former is that of reincarnation, touched on briefly in "To Our Ladies of Death" and expanded only a little more fully here. That Thomson saw fit to expand it at all at this later date should not, however, be taken as significant; the idea is presented as a picture, the flat monotony and unvarying rhythm of which gives rise to idle wondering but not to considered thought. The other of these earlier ideas is that of pantheism, already pointed out in "The Doom" and "A Happy Poet." The expression of it in "A Lady" differs from the earlier expressions only in a slight shift of emphasis from the concept of a universal soul to the promise of immortality that lies in that concept.

The second and more important group of ideas in this section of "A Lady" Thomson had first expressed in a somewhat hesitant, incomplete form in "Our Ladies of Death"; in the phantasy he developed them more fully and expressed them with more sureness. The first of these ideas he derived from the law of the indestructibility of matter: however great may be the physical changes of a substance, every atom of it remains in existence throughout all time. Thus, that which is commonly called the mortal body is in truth immortal. Again and again in the course of his life, Thomson insisted on this concept of immortality. In "Our Ladies of Death," he had written,

> One part of me shall feed a little worm,
> And it a bird on which a man may feed;

In "A Lady of Sorrow" he put the same thought into prose: "Let no atom in the world be proud; it is now in the heart of a hero, it may soon be in a serpent's fang. Let no atom in the world be ashamed; it is now in the refuse of a dung-hill, it may soon be in the loveliest leaf of a rose."

The second major idea is that of the omnipotence and unconsciousness of the laws of nature. This idea Thomson handled in different ways in his writings but always as it related to man. In "The Doom" he had expressed the thesis that nature was indifferent to man; in "Vane's Story" he had emphasized the impotence of man under such laws; in "A Lady" he stressed man's insignificance in a universe so ruled. Far from being the center of the universe for whom all things were created, man he now saw as a small and unimportant step in a great order prescribed by the laws of the universe.

> When will you freely and gladly own the truth that whatever is born in Time must decay and perish in Time? As your race studies fossil relics of plant and shell and gigantic animal, so shall future existences (to you in their kind inconceivable) study fossil relics of your race.

This concept of man's place in the universe clearly appealed to Thomson, for he expressed it repeatedly and frequently in his later writings.

In addition to the mood and the philosophic ideas presented in "A Lady," the phantasy shows a trait of Thomson's character exhibited throughout his work, though difficult to document by line reference, a trait related equally to his analytical thinking and his imaginative sympathy. In one of the finest prose passages he ever wrote he insisted on his agnosticism: "Know this only, that you can never know; of this only be assured, that you shall never be assured; doubt not that you must doubt to the end—if ever end there be. . . ." Despite his various assertions of atheistic beliefs, this creed he held, both intellectually and emotionally, to be more nearly true than any other. And that he did hold it and permitted it to exercise a restraining influence on his mind and work at all times saved his writings from dogmatism. It is true that he codified his beliefs and wrote of them as though they were indisputable facts; but no passage in his work, however intense in feeling, however positive in form, makes the reader feel that he is being shouted at. Sympathy and tolerance pervade even the most arbitrary sections. It is this attitude of moderation that makes incorrect the use of the word *atheist;* Thomson was not an atheist, he was an agnostic.

During these four years that Thomson lived with the Bradlaughs his dipsomania grew steadily worse and by 1863 he had become too much affected to hold a steady position.[38] No details, such as events or moods preceding the attacks or even their frequency, are available, however, for both Salt and Dobell, the only biographers who might have found evidence, treated Thomson's disease as briefly as possible. Both

---

[38] Hypatia Bradlaugh Bonner, *Charles Bradlaugh,* I, 109–113. Mrs. Bonner's remarks must be taken with qualifications, for she was writing after Thomson's quarrel with her father, when she had turned against the poet most bitterly and was clearly unfair in her judgments. She stated, for example, that Thomson was drinking very heavily at this time; but she was a child of only eight or nine when he left the household and it seems likely, therefore, that she was generalizing freely from a few incidents which had especially impressed her. The amount of work that Thomson turned out during this period seems to me to offer strong evidence that, though he may have suffered occasional attacks, he did not have them as often as she implied nor become as irregular as she stated. But from the documentary evidence that she offered, it is sure that the disease was gaining ground.

recognized dipsomania as a disease but they feared, justly as subsequent events proved, sensationalism.

In October, 1866, Thomson left the Bradlaugh home. It is difficult to explain the move; apparently he was as happy there as he could be anywhere; certainly there was no disagreement between him and any member of the house, for he saw much of the family after his departure. Why then he should have gone to live in a cheap furnished room, barren and cheerless, is hard to understand. Mrs. Bradlaugh shared to some degree Thomson's weakness, and her daughter charged that her fight against intemperance was defeated by convivial friends. Whether there is any connection between her drinking, Thomson's dipsomania, and his leaving the Bradlaugh home, I cannot state as a fact, but it is a possible explanation. Thomson may have felt that his influence was bad, Bradlaugh may have suggested that it was and in all friendliness requested him to leave, or Mrs. Bradlaugh herself may have felt that his presence made her struggle more difficult. In any case he left.

And his departure marks the end of this period in his life. It was, as I have noted, a period of great creative vitality during which he wrote satiric and nonsatiric essays, tried his skill at fiction, expanded his field of translation, produced the Cockney poetry, and wrote the personal, philosophic "Vane's Story" and "A Lady of Sorrow." And in several of these genres he did excellent work. Yet it was not a period of maturity but rather one of continuing development, of preparation. There are too many threads in the pattern to weave together here, but a few of those noted in the preceding period and leading to "The City of Dreadful Night" in the next period may be traced briefly. The somewhat general dissatisfaction with life which Thomson had expressed during his army days in the poem written on his twenty-third birthday shows in this early London period in the theories expressed in "Per Contra" and in the aloof approach of the Cockney poems as dissatisfaction with the life of a writer; in "The City of Dreadful Night" it will be seen as bitter disappointment with the life he himself had lived. The longing for certainty, observed in the works of the army period, especially in such a poem as "Mater Tenebrarum," does not appear in the writings of these years, nor is the note of doubt any longer clear; but the compromise personal religion, seen earlier in "The Doom of a City," "Shelley," and many other poems, remains though expressed less frequently. It ends, however, soon after "A Lady of Sorrow," at the close of this period, and the way is opened for the final steps in Thomson's philosophy as found in "The City of Dreadful Night." The highly personal sentimentalism of the early Matilda poems, such as "Love's Dawn," "The Fadeless Bower," and "Parting," had given way even before Thomson came to London to a mellower, less personal, more philosophic attitude in "Our Ladies of Death." His philosophic interests had appeared also in the army period in "The Doom." In this early London period the philosophic concepts of these two poems are repeated in a more developed form in "Vane's Story" and "A Lady of Sorrow," in both of which Matilda and Thomson's grief still appear, now balanced by the philosophic elements. These works will in turn lead to "The City of Dreadful Night," where (except for one section) the Matilda elements will be absorbed by the philosophic. Thus may be roughly traced the continuity of both Thomson's life and his works.

# CHAPTER III

# The City

## 1866-1873

THOMSON'S love of the country appears in the descriptions of Jersey scenery in "Ronald and Helen," some of the lyrics of "Sunday up the River" and "Sunday at Hampstead," his letters from America, his articles on Spain, his accounts of the Barrs home in the country, where he spent much time shortly before his death, and in others of his works and letters. The countryside gave him a sense of freedom, expressed in his comparison of the two army camps of Aldershot and Curragh:

> Aldershot is set amidst dark heath, the Curragh amidst green grass; and the difference is like that between cloudy and sunshiny weather. It is good to get out here from a town. The sky is seen, not in patches, but broad, complete, and sea-like; the distance where low blue hills float in the horizon is also sea-like, and the uncorrupted air sweeps over us broad and free as an ocean.[1]

---

[1] Salt, *op. cit.*, p. 33.

Yet when he went from the Bradlaugh home in Tottenham to live in Pimlico, between the Victoria Station and the river, he left a villa almost in the country for a room in a densely populated section of London, only a few blocks from main business streets, where the rows and rows of three- and four-story houses were built the one against the other, their doors separated from the sidewalk only by areaways, where the only openness was an occasional tree-filled square.[2]

He left also the home of a family of which he was a part for a room in a house occupied by strangers who, although under the same roof, neither knew nor cared, as he became painfully aware, whether he was dead or alive. The bleak loneliness he experienced in these quarters he described in the autobiographical poem, "In the Room," 1867–1868. In a drab chamber with a "chilly hearth and naked floor," the pieces of furniture converse about him. The cupboard complains that it gets no more than a pinch of meal and a crust all the week long; and the mirror grumbles that the Man is not so gay and happy as the previous tenant, Lucy, and that last night he was pale, his eyes were too bright, and he muttered bad words. The table sighs that it grows weary of his weight as he writes endlessly, and the grate responds peevishly that his labor is all futile since he burns everything he writes. The mirror again grumbles:

> . . . Write and write!
> And read those stupid, worn-out books!
> That's all he does, read, write, and read,
> And smoke that nasty pipe which stinks:

> .    .    .

---

[2] After an initial period on Denbigh Street, Thomson lived for some three years at 69 Warwick Street and then moved to 240 Vauxhall Bridge Road (*ibid.*, p. 57).

But with this dullard, glum and sour,
  Not one of all his fellow-men
Has ever passed a social hour;
  We might be in some wild beast's den.

The bed then startles them with the quiet announcement
that the Man lies dead upon it; and the vial adds that he had
drunk its contents of poison. In such lodgings, where Thomson felt the very furniture was more concerned with him than
were human beings, he came to understand a line from one
of the Leopardi letters he translated: "In brief, solitude is not
made for those who burn and consume themselves by themselves."

Financial insecurity, which Thomson had not hitherto experienced but from which he was never again to escape, also
began to threaten. When, in 1870, Bradlaugh turned the
*National Reformer* over to his assistants, Thomson felt unsure
of a market for his work although it actually continued to
appear as regularly as before, and he therefore sought a sup-
plementary means of livelihood of which he could be more
certain. For a while he worked in a printing office, reading
proof, revising copy, and doing similar tasks. Then he became
secretary to a commercial company, which shortly went out
of business. The same thing happened a second time, and
then a third. The truth of the matter was, apparently, that no
established business concern could afford to hire a man who
was known to be so irregular as Thomson's more and more
frequent attacks of dipsomania made him. The letter he wrote
describing the situation, though light and gay, sounds a note,
not yet of anxiety, but of uneasiness.[3] Thus to his loneliness
was added financial worry.

---

[3] Letter to Mrs. John Thomson, January 1, 1872, quoted by Salt, *op. cit.*,
pp. 65–67.

Such circumstances were naturally conducive to the fits of depression to which Thomson was always subject. The nature of the depression in the earlier years and its relation to his religious doubts is indicated to some extent in "The Doom" and more fully in "Vane's Story"; but its character in these and later years is less surely defined, for Thomson no longer made direct reference to it. There remains, however, a diary entry, quoted by Salt, showing the vague feeling of apathetic despair which characterized at least one day, and probably many more, in this period:

> Sunday, November 4, 1869.—Burned all my old papers, manuscripts, and letters, save the book MSS. which have been already in great part printed. It took me five hours to burn them, guarding against chimney on fire, and keeping them thoroughly burning. I was sad and stupid—scarcely looked into any; had I begun reading them, I might never have finished their destruction. All the letters; those which I had kept for twenty years, those which I had kept for more than sixteen. I felt myself like one who, having climbed half-way up a long rope (35 on the 23rd inst.), cuts off all beneath his feet; he must climb on, and can never touch the old earth again without a fatal fall. The memories treasured in the letters can never, at least in great part, be revived in my life again, nor in the lives of the friends yet living who wrote them. But after this terrible year, I could do no less than consume the past. I can now better face the future, come in what guise it may.[4]

What made 1869 "this terrible year" is not known, nor can the friends who wrote the letters Thomson had kept for

---

[4] Salt, *op. cit.*, pp. 58–59.

twenty years be identified; but it was sixteen years and a few months since Matilda's death and doubtless some of the letters he refrained from reading as he shoved them into the flames in his little fireplace were from her.

As Thomson continued to live in London, the city itself came to exercise an almost hypnotic emotional effect on him. This becomes apparent in certain aspects of Thomson's life and writings during these and later years: the apathetic quality of the depression noted in the above-quoted diary entry; the intensely personal feeling in the sections of "The City of Dreadful Night" dealing with the City itself; Thomson's reactions to America and Spain and his immediate return to his old life on coming back to London; his response, a re-awakening of his creative abilities, to the country life given him by the Barrs during his last year of life. At first London had seemed merely cold and unsympathetic, as in "In the Room." Then gradually he became aware of the ruthless quality of its tremendous size and its relentlessly steady march. As he walked along the river or up Whitehall Street, he sought in the faces of those he met a spirit of friendliness or a glow of happiness. But every man seemed like himself, dull and despairing and alone, and he recognized the insignificance and helplessness of the little human cogs in London's un-ceasing, unconscious machinery. The city became for him the City of Dreadful Night, as its net of despair and loneliness enveloped him and atrophied his hope. He came to think of London as the home of the lonely and the hopeless, who made up the fraternity of which he was becoming a member. It was not that the city was simply unaware of him—it was as though it were a malignant force asserting its emotional domination over him, a curse which half paralyzed him and left him with no vitality to fight.

There were thousands and thousands of human kind
   In this desert of brick and stone:
But some were deaf and some were blind,
   And he was there alone.[5]

A survey of Thomson's work during these years from 1866 to 1873 shows that most of the basic elements noted in the previous period continue but that the pattern is slightly different. The satires are fewer in number and different in subject. The personal essays, such as "Per Contra" and "Open Secret Societies," are replaced by informative essays,[6] based on research, whose chief significance is that they are the first examples of a form of journalism which Thomson was to employ extensively at a later date. The impulse to write narrative appeared in poetry rather than in prose. Translations occupied a larger amount of his time and interest and a position of greater importance in his total output. And finally, the philosophic writing culminated in "The City of Dreadful Night."

Even as the satires of Thomson's early London period fell into two groups, the religious and the nonreligious, so do those of these years fall into two classes, the political and the nonpolitical. In the former group there are two essays, "Commission of Inquiry as to Complaints against Royalty" and "A Bible Lesson on Monarchy," both 1870, and three epigrams, "We Croak," 1871, "Poor Indeed!" 1871, and "Our Congratulations on the Recovery of His Royal Highness," 1872. Comparable in tone and method to the religious satires, they attack the monarchy. Typical is the epigram "We Croak":

---

[5] "William Blake," in "The Poems of William Blake."
[6] The informative essays included "Paul Louis Courier," "Paul Louis Courier on the Land Question," "Paul Louis Courier on the Character of the People," "Marcus Aurelius Antonius," etc.

When Stork succeeded Log as King
The poor frogs fared but ill;
We've both at once—the senseless thing,
The damnable long bill.

The reason for the new subject is clear and significant. With the fall of Napoleon III in 1870 and the establishment of a republican government in France, republicanism became for a short period a popular issue in England, one of the most emphasized of the arguments for which was the expense of maintaining the royal family with its "damnable long bill." Bradlaugh embraced the cause enthusiastically and "thundered against 'princely paupers' to one of the largest crowds that had ever been seen in Trafalgar Square. . . ." [7] Thus in attacking the monarch Thomson was but following the lead of his editor. That he sincerely believed in the evils of monarchy and the virtues of republicanism cannot be doubted when one reads the earlier "L'Ancien Régime," a bitterly satiric poem of 1867, or his letter from America on Americans; [8] yet realizing that his writing of first the religious satires and then the political satires coincided with Bradlaugh's interests of the moment enables one to judge more accurately the weight these should be given in a consideration of his works. That he honestly held the ideas he expressed is sure; that they were important enough to him to express had he not been writing for the *National Reformer* is open to question.

The nonpolitical satires show no such relation to the *National Reformer* and are, therefore, a more interesting group. The first of these is "Indolence: A Moral Essay," 1867. Rich

---

[7] Strachey, *Queen Victoria*, pp. 338 ff. See also Bradlaugh's *Impeachment of the House of Brunswick*, 1872.

[8] Quoted later in this chapter.

with well-chosen and skillfully handled literary allusion, it is an analysis of the various types of indolence and a hearty commendation of all, pleasant reading with its mood of quietly happy relaxation and amusement.[9] The second, "A National Reformer in the Dog Days," 1869, is an argument that it is more logical to lie under a tree and sing the praises of the reformers who toil and sweat than it is to join them in their folly.[10] And the third is the whimsical "Proposals for the Speedy Extinction of Evil and Misery," 1868, 1871, which derives its quiet humor from the exaggerated seriousness with which Thomson reduced to absurdity popular plans for reform by pushing them to their logical conclusions and then, with an ostentatious display of illogicalness, presented his own plan. This is not one of Thomson's better satires. Running to fifty-two pages, it is too long, too detailed, and it lacks the quick, incisive, suggestive strokes that characterized even the longest of the religious satires, "The Story of a Famous Old Firm" (sixteen pages long). In fact none of these finds a place among Thomson's better satires, yet the three are unique in that they alone of his prose satires express any of his philosophic ideas. Very briefly in "Indolence," more fully in "A National Reformer," and very completely in "Proposals" he

---

[9] On this essay I disagree with Salt, *op. cit.,* pp. 271–272, who wrote that "Indolence" "is yet another illustration of Thomson's hatred of that spirit of busybodyism and proselytism which would interfere with the natural bent of the individual mind" and who goes on to overemphasize the philosophic element of the essay by quoting in full the single paragraph in which it is expressed. In this instance, I feel, Salt has fallen into one of the categories at which Thomson pokes fun, the "Earnest."

[10] Again I disagree with Salt, *loc. cit.,* who feels that "A National Reformer" is more humorous than "Indolence." I can say only that it was obviously intended to be more humorous.

says that man, being subject to the omnipotent laws of nature, is not able to help himself.

Before leaving the satires it is necessary to mention one more, a poem, "Supplement to the Inferno," 1870. Most of Thomson's satiric work, both prose and poetry, is almost playful and shows a spirit of tolerant amusement and good-natured mockery; but in the "Supplement" the gentle irony gives way to biting satire and the tolerant, amused note is replaced by one of vulgarity and ugliness. Only two other times did he write anything approaching this in character, "A Real Vision of Sin," 1859, and "L'Ancien Régime," 1867, above noted. But the earlier of these, written, according to a marginal note on the manuscript, "in disgust at Tennyson's which is very pretty and clever and silly and truthless," shares with the "Supplement" only ugliness; and the latter has in common with it only an almost passionate vehemence. Moreover the "Vision" was directed against what Thomson felt to be the superficiality of a concept and "L'Ancien Régime" against an institution, whereas the "Supplement" was a personal attack on an individual, Bulwer-Lytton, whom Thomson despised as he despised no other man. The following passage illustrates the character of the poem. "The thing," Lytton, is reciting his earthly achievements to Minos, who sits in judgment. Minos interrupts:

> . . . Be damned! Great Jove, did e'er one see a
> Creature like this 'mong men or beasts or birds?
> A dictionary with the diarrhoea
> Could hardly spout such feculent flux of words.

There is no sure explanation for the savageness Thomson displayed in this poem. There is, however, a reasonable one.

According to Salt, there was a rumor that Thomson was the illegitimate son of Bulwer-Lytton.[11] Surely he must have hated such a rumor and desired to indicate what he thought of both the man and the gossip, yet his doing so in such a manner seems inconsistent with the Thomson we know. It may be assumed, therefore, that he was at the time suffering the excessive irritability common among nerve-taut dipsomaniacs, and that in this condition he conceived and, in furious haste, wrote the piece. This explanation would account for the angry satire of the quick and apparently effortless poem and is consistent with some of his actions during quarrels with Bradlaugh and Foote at a later date.

To turn from this satire to Thomson's narrative poetry of the period is to turn from a mood of savagery to one approaching sentimentality. "Two Lovers," 1867, is a simple romantic tale, simply told, concerning a Mohammedan man and a Christian girl. Separated in life by their religions, each on his deathbed changes his faith that they may be united in heaven. The story ends with verses which express again Thomson's belief in the value of a full life and recall to the reader both the idea of and the method employed in Browning's "The Statue and the Bust":

> Love out your cordial love, hate out your hate;
>     Be strong to grasp a foe, to clasp a friend;
>   Your wants true laws are; thirst and hunger sate:
>     Feel you have been yourselves when comes the end.

The second of the narrative poems, the Oriental "Weddah and Om-el-Bonain," 1868–1869, is a much longer work with a

---

[11] Both Salt and William Sharp denied any element of truth in the story, and the entry in the parish register at Edinburgh, quoted in Chapter I, seems final proof of the falsity of it.

more fully developed plot expanded with greater detail; yet
it moves quickly and without undue digression. While Weddah is fighting his tribal enemies, Om-el-Bonain is persuaded
to marry the chief of a third tribe to gain his support for her
people. On her sweetheart's return from the wars, she hides
him in a chest. The husband, informed of the affair, has the
unopened chest buried and shortly thereafter the girl dies
over the grave. The plots for both poems Thomson took from
Stendhal's "De l'Amour," expanding and elaborating them.[12]

"Weddah and Om-el-Bonain" was highly praised by William M. Rossetti when Thomson sent him a copy and again
later, when it appeared in the volume, *Vane's Story and Other
Poems,* by both Meredith and Swinburne. And certainly no
other of Thomson's works received such fulsome commenda-
tions from the reviewers and critics as did this. True it is that
some of the descriptive passages have genuine lyrical quality,
but the poem as a whole fails, in my opinion, for the same
reason that Thomson's fiction failed: the characters are so
wooden that the reader feels no sympathy with them and does
not respond to them. Again the fact that Thomson was interested chiefly in ideas is apparent, and in this instance it
is emphasized by a comparison of "Weddah" and "Two
Lovers." The latter, which is inferior in many respects, is the

---

[12] In an introductory note to the poem Thomson wrote, "I found this
story ['Weddah'], and that of the shorter piece following ['Two Lovers'],
which merit far better English versions than I have been able to accomplish, in the *De l'Amour* of De Stendhal (Henri Beyle), chapt. 53. . . ."
But Thomson actually gave more than mere "versions" of these two
stories. To the former he added the circumstances of Weddah's absence
at the time of Om-el-Bonain's marriage, his return and sorrow, and her
letter to him, making a poem of a thousand lines out of Stendhal's bare
750 words. And from the latter story of some 150 words, he made a
poem of eighty-eight lines, adding to it thirty-six more lines of philosophy.

more effective, because Thomson was using his story to illustrate an idea. When his story was subordinate to an idea, he was able to handle it; but when it had to stand alone, he fumbled.

Far superior to these narrative poems, indeed superior to all but a small handful that he ever wrote, is the strange autobiographical poem, "In the Room," 1867–1868, of which I have given a synopsis early in this chapter. Its tone is consistent throughout, and the suspense is well handled, with a good build-up and a careful, restrained climax. The poem is simple and straightforward in structure, expression, and development; at the same time it is dramatically effective. The character of the Man, skillfully drawn by contrasting him with the Girl, is vivid; and the furniture, none of which is given a physical description, is given personality and vitality. But the poem's highest quality is its personal effect on the reader. Thomson gave only a few descriptive details, but he chose provocative ones which stimulate the reader's imagination to supply the rest. He visualizes the room, and it becomes his own. Thus he shares with Thomson the loneliness, the sense of being so cut off from human intercourse that only the furniture knows that he is dead—knows or cares. This is indeed one of Thomson's masterpieces.

But more significant in these years immediately preceding the writing of "The City of Dreadful Night" than the satires, than the narrative poems, even than "In the Room," is, I think, Thomson's work on Leopardi. When his interest in that Italian philosopher was aroused is not at all sure. Dobell suggested that it may have been in the early 1860's, for it was sometime between the years 1862 and 1866 that Thomson began his study of the Italian language, but there is no clear evidence for this supposition.[13] At any rate he was a student of Leopardi by the end of 1867, when his first translation, "Copernicus," appeared in the *National Reformer*. Within a year he had published twelve translations; [14] and in the last months of 1869 and the first of 1870 he had written some hundred pages of an essay on Leopardi, for which he had read the six hundred fifty letters of the *Epistolario* and made translations of many.[15] Thus one may be sure that during these years a major part of his time and energy went into the study of the Italian pessimist.

That this preoccupation with Leopardi showed in "The

---

[13] Dobell, "Introduction" to Thomson's translation of Leopardi, *Essays, Dialogues and Thoughts*, p. x.

[14] Of the twenty-eight items in the index of Thomson's translations as printed by Routledge, twelve appeared in the *National Reformer* in 1867–1868. The remaining sixteen, to judge by diary entries of the later years, were done between 1874 and 1877; an entry of November 15, 1877, notes that on that date he finished the "Operette Morali." These latter sixteen Thomson translated completely but did not revise. After his death Dobell reworked them from the manuscripts and prepared them for publication. So successful was he that, without his notes, the reader would be unable to distinguish between those finished by Thomson himself and those revised by Dobell.

[15] The essay was to have consisted of three parts: a memoir or biographical sketch of Leopardi's life; notes on his works of general interest; and finally, "remarks on his genius and philosophy." The memoir, which consists almost entirely of translated selections of the *Epistolario* chosen so that Leopardi's life is told directly in his own words with only occasional remarks and short paragraphs by Thomson to bridge the gaps, was completed, and the first fifty-seven and a half pages of the essay as they stand in the Routledge edition were printed in the *National Reformer* in late 1869 and early 1870. The remaining thirty-one, appended to the first in the Routledge edition without a break, were not printed in Thomson's life. The second part of the essay, the notes on the works, was apparently never even started; but the third part was at least begun, or at least it is assumed that that fragment published under the title "Parallel beween Pascal and Leopardi" in the Routledge edition was to have been a portion of the third part.

City" in phrases and lines is not to be disputed; indeed, Thomson himself called attention to his literary debt to Leopardi, and also to Dante, by prefacing the poem with quotations from their works. But to explore this debt is not my purpose. I am interested rather in a problem I consider more significant: what if any influence Leopardi had on Thomson's thinking and what might be the relation between Thomson's work on Leopardi and his starting "The City."

Because the date of his first reading of Leopardi cannot be positively established, it is impossible to state definitely that Thomson entertained certain ideas prior to it, but the probability can be determined. There is good evidence he started his study of Italian not earlier than 1862—Dobell suggested "1864 or thereabouts"—at a time when no English translation of Leopardi existed. Moreover, according to the *British Museum Catalogue of Printed Books,* 1890, the only French translation in print was *Les Chants de Leopardi,* 1853. The German translations, *Gedichte* and *Dichtungen,* were later, 1866 and 1869 respectively. And before any of these dates except that of *Les Chants,* Thomson had already expressed, though with hesitancy, it is to be admitted, the ideas of the disregard of nature for man, the insignificance of man, and the laws of nature in "The Doom of a City," 1857, and "To Our Ladies of Death," 1861. And these ideas he expanded and emphasized in "A Lady of Sorrow," 1862–1864, and "Vane's Story," 1864, the earliest dates at which there is even reasonable possibility that he might have started reading Leopardi.[16] Thus the probability is strong that Thomson

---

[16] The use of the name *Leopardi* in the fragmentary narrative cannot be used as evidence since the story is undated and the pianist bearing the name shows no characteristic in common with the philosopher.

quite independently held these ideas, basic in both his and Leopardi's philosophy, before he made the acquaintance of the Italian pessimist. It is also reasonable to think that when Thomson did start reading Leopardi he became interested not because he found new ideas, but because he discovered affirmation of his own. And it may well have been this affirmation, this authority, which so strengthened and encouraged him in his ideas that he started "The City"; that work on it followed so closely on the heels of work on Leopardi may have been no coincidence. As I have commented earlier, agreement can be a potent force.

Thomson worked on Leopardi into the year 1870, and it was in 1870 that he started "The City of Dreadful Night." How much of it he wrote before laying it aside for some two years is impossible to say; he himself said only, "About half of it, and not the first half as it now stands, was written in 1870; and then it was not touched till 1873, when I roughly finished it, licking it into shape at the beginning of the present year [1874]." [17] Even more difficult to ascertain is why he started it at the time he did. The long development toward it is easily traced from "The Doom" and "To Our Ladies of Death," through "A Lady of Sorrow" and "Vane's Story," to the Leopardi translations and essay. The character necessary to the writing of such a poem, sympathetic and imaginative, analytical and intellectually honest, is clear. The conduciveness of his emotional state—his loneliness, his depression, his feeling of insecurity—is apparent. And the environment, the London which intensified his depression till it took on the qualities of a narcotic, is right. But the

---

[17] Quoted by Salt, *op. cit.*, p. 109.

catalytic agent which made these elements become active and demand expression is not known nor are there data which permit even a guess. One knows the preparation for "The City" but not its immediate cause. It is possible only to quote from one of Thomson's later works:

> Long poems, indeed, are usually premeditated and planned in their general outline; but the first conception of the subject, in its most general outline, yet most essential living individuality, must be as unpremeditated, as real a lightning-flash of inspiration as ever suddenly illumined mystic or seer. Moreover, many of the details, whether of episode or organic development, many of the noblest passages, whether for beauty or energy, must be just as unpremeditated, just as unexpectedly inspired. And beyond doubt, many of the loveliest lyrics and brief poems have been poured forth in a single sudden jet, like metal at a white heat in the intolerable fire of inspiration, swift as a thunderbolt from a quiet sky. . . .[18]

Suddenly in 1872, when Thomson's lonely life in London seemed set in a rigid pattern of hopelessness, an exciting and stimulating new adventure opened up to him, one which offered both escape and fresh interests. The Champion Gold and Silver Company, of which he was secretary, sent him to America. He left London on April 27, and a month later was in the mining town of Central City, Colorado.[19]

Colorado offered much to stimulate Thomson. The vastness and roughness of the country were exhilarating to a poet who had known no wilder scenery than Dublin's low, rolling

---

[18] "A Strange Book," 1879.
[19] Salt, *op. cit.*, p. 77.

hills and Jersey's lush valleys and rocky coast. Thomson wrote with zest of the Rocky Mountains, "the big vertebrae of this longish backbone of America," and of dramatic lightning storms. Even the ugly little town interested him, for he sensed, as he looked at the surrounding mountains, "scarred and gashed and ulcerated all over from past mining operations," a dynamic force in the group of untidy rough wood houses huddled at the bottom of the ravine.[20] But what most impressed and stimulated Thomson was the vitality and confidence and ambition of these western Americans, attitudes so unlike those he had held in London. And, alive to all impressions, sympathetic to every mood, he himself began to share the energy and eagerness of these people. This new vigor is noticeable in many of his letters from America, but especially in one from which the following is taken:

> [The Americans] are intoxicated with their vast country and its vaster prospects. . . . The Americans of today are only a nation in that they instinctively adore their Union. All the heterogeneous ingredients are seething in the cauldron with plenty of scum and air-bubbles atop. In a century or two they may get stewed down into homogeneity—a really wholesome and dainty dish, not to be set before a king though, I fancy. I resisted the impression of mere material vastitude as long as possible, but found its influence growing on me week by week; for it implies such vast possibilities of moral and intellectual expansion. They are starting over here with all our experience and culture at their command, without any of the obsolete burdens and impediments which

---

[20] Letter to William M. Rossetti, August 5, 1872, quoted by Salt, *op. cit.*, pp. 82–89.

in the course of a thousand years have become insepara-
ble from our institutions, and with a country which will
want more labour and more people for many generations
to come.[21]

But Thomson was not to enjoy his new energy and eagerness for long, was not to have the opportunity of probing
America's "vast possibilities of moral and intellectual expan-
sion." Late in the year he was recalled and was back in London
by the end of January, 1873.[22] His expenses, both for traveling
and living, were paid by the company, but he received only
a small part of his salary, the contract having been verbal
and apparently not properly authorized.[23] To be unpaid was
a disappointment, but more disappointing was the failure of
the position to fulfill its promise of a new life in a new country.
He wrote on his return to England, "I enjoyed my trip to

---

[21] Published in the *Secular Review,* July 15, 1882.

[22] During Thomson's stay in Central City the old Log-cabin Theater,
built in 1860, was the center of the mining town's cultural life;
but in 1874 it, along with the rest of the town, burned down. In 1878,
however, it was replaced by the still standing Central City Opera
House. As the boom days of Central City passed, the Opera House fell
into disrepair and became "the famous 'Ghost Theater' of the vanished
west." In time it was presented to the University of Denver and work
on restoration was started. It was then discovered that the original
handmade hickory chairs were in good condition, so, to finance the work,
they were "sold" at $100 each as memorials to the early settlers, each so
sold to be carved with the name of the pioneer and with the date of
his arrival in Colorado. One such in the Opera House now bears the
name of James Thomson. In connection with the Opera House there is
published a book titled *The Glory That Was Gold.* This contains, in
addition to a short history of the theater, from which the above information was taken, one-page biographies of each of those for whom a chair
was named. The authors of these sketches are not indicated, but the
namers of the chairs are; it was Dixon Wecter who named the Thomson
chair.

[23] Salt, *op. cit.,* p. 93.

America very much, and should like to be sent out there again. If I were only about twenty years old, or if, old as I am, I had a good trade, I would certainly emigrate and become a citizen of the free and enlightened Republic." [24]

That he was thirty-eight and without confidence that in the United States he could earn even such a meager living as he did in England was doubtless his own reason for not returning to America; but there was, I think, a more fundamental one. On his return to London Thomson, resuming the routine he had followed before his trip, slipped swiftly and completely into his customary habits. Emotionally and intellectually he fell back into the old pattern, uninfluenced permanently by his more recent experiences. His writing was not affected by so much as the addition of fresh material. [25] The journey had been but a brief interruption. That he thus returned to his old life without making any effort to escape from it, without even realizing, apparently, that it was possible to escape from it, is at the same time the result and evidence of the hypnotic, stupefying spell which London seemed to cast over him. Back in quarters similar to those of "In the Room," he immediately fell prey again to the city, the City of Dreadful Night, and its numbing despair, breeder of apathy. The extent to which

---

[24] Letter to Hypatia Bradlaugh, February 28, 1873, quoted by Salt, *op. cit.*, pp. 95–96.

[25] The only work which bears more than a casual reference to America is "Religion in the Rocky Mountains," 1873, a satire similar to the earlier ones, which utilizes a few American place names and colloquialisms. It shows, however, no significant influence of his experiences. A second example of the use of the American scene has been suggested by critics who note that the brief description of the mountains rising behind the City of Dreadful Night (section i of "The City") may have been inspired by the Rocky Mountains; it is as likely, however, since Thomson worked on "The City" while in Spain, that the scene was suggested by the Pyrenees.

this spell sapped his initiative is indicated by the unintention-
ally revealing choice of words in the letter above quoted: "I
. . . should like *to be sent* out there again." [26]

Six months after his return Thomson was granted a second
reprieve. He accepted a position as special correspondent to
the *New York World,* in which capacity he went to Spain
late in July, 1873, to report the activities of the Carlists, who
were rebelling against the newly formed and short-lived
republic.[27] Thomson and his employers expected that he
would see sharp fighting, but only occasionally was there so
much as a desultory skirmish. Consequently he had ample
time to enjoy the beauty of the countryside with its poplars
and flowers, the sturdy peasants who had forced Don Carlos
to respect their rights before they would give him their support, and the cordial villagers who arranged elaborate enter-
tainments of singing and dancing for the troops. Even the
army life was agreeable: the marches were slow and easy, the
siestas were long, and the evenings spent conversing with
the other correspondents and English-speaking Carlist troops
were pleasant.[28] This indolent, carefree existence he found
relaxing and happy.

But Thomson was not allowed to remain happy long. Early
in September he collapsed under the hot sun of Spain,[29] and

---

[26] Italics are mine.

[27] Salt, *op. cit.,* p. 98.

[28] Thomson described this life in a series of four articles titled "Carlist
Reminiscences," which appeared in *The Secularist* March 11, 18, 25,
and April 1, 1876. It is unfortunate that these, better written and more
interesting than many of his works which have been reprinted, remain
unreprinted except for the selection from the second article quoted by
Salt, *op. cit.,* pp. 99–100.

[29] Thomson was ill for three days at Alsasua and again for ten at San
Estevan. Mrs. Bonner in her biography of her father hinted that Thomson

for two weeks he lay on his cot, miserable and lonely, fearing that he, like Heine, was doomed to spend the rest of his days on a "mattress-grave." [30] As the days dragged by he apparently began to realize that, because he had sent but little copy to his employers, he would shortly be recalled to London, that this escape from the City had also failed.[31] These glorious, lazy days with the delightful Basque people were no more than a brief holiday; they could not last. It was as though the City were reaching with long tentacles, even to Spain, to torment him and drag him back. Sick and disheartened, his hopes defeated, he began again to work in his mind on "The City of Dreadful Night." [32]

At about the time he became ill he did indeed receive his recall, having contributed only three letters. He was back in London late in September, almost two months after he had left, where once again he was refused his salary. He protested that he could not send in news stories when there was no news. Mrs. Bonner, however, maintained that "as a climax he wrote three lines describing an important event when three columns were expected." Whatever the truth was, the fact remained that he failed to receive the five pounds a week that had been promised him.[33]

---

was not suffering from sunstroke but from another attack of dipsomania. Considering, however, the animus she frequently displayed towards Thomson in that book and the undeniable fact that on his return to London he suffered poorer health than he had ever before known, one discounts her implication.

[30] This phrase, borrowed from Heine himself, apparently haunted Thomson, for he had used it nearly ten years earlier in "Vane's Story."

[31] Salt, *op. cit.*, p. 101, wrote "On September 3 Thomson received the expected letter of recall. . . ."

[32] Salt, 1914 edition, p. 71.

[33] Salt, *op. cit.*, pp. 101–102.

The financial disappointment was the more serious because of his inability to find employment for some time; as long as two months after his return he wrote that he was still unsuccessful, ". . . though, of course, I have been making every effort." Moreover his health was poor, as it was to be for the rest of his life, and he suffered for several weeks from an eye infection which prevented him from reading, writing, and even smoking. It is little wonder that he was extremely depressed.[34] It was at this time that he finished "The City of Dreadful Night." [35]

The importance of "The City of Dreadful Night" to students of nineteenth-century thought cannot be easily over-estimated. A number of Victorian writers, their faith attacked by the new scientific knowledge and its mechanistic implications, were forced to question the importance of man in the universe, and the answer at which many of them arrived left them disillusioned. As a result, there is a large body of Victorian literature which is marked in varying degrees by disappointment, depression, and even pessimism. Arnold expressed it emotionally in "Dover Beach"; Tennyson, vacillating, uncertain, voiced it hesitantly in "In Memoriam"; Clough put it into words in "Perchè Pensa? Pensando s'invecchia." But no one expressed it so clearly, so deeply, so unfalteringly as did Thomson in "The City." Because "The City" is the most complete articulation of this pessimism, its value as an index

---

[34] Letters to Alice Bradlaugh, November 24, 1873, quoted by Salt, *op. cit.,* p. 104; and to Bertram Dobell, October 9, 1880, quoted by Salt, *op. cit.,* pp. 155–156.

[35] October, November, and December, 1873, Thomson spent writing the rough draft of the remaining sections. January and February, 1874, he polished, revised, and prepared the poem for publication.

to the thinking of the Victorian men of letters is great.

That it is so does not mean, however, that "The City" is dated, that it is a phenomenon of the Victorian period alone. The mood of disillusionment is one which has been common to thinkers of a certain temperament in all countries in all times. It is found alike in Sophocles and T. S. Eliot. There have always been, and probably always will be, men who have had faith, who have lost that faith and with it hope, and who have despaired. There have been men who doubt that there is any ultimate good in the universe, who believe that man is impotent, who find no answer to the query, "Why were we born?" And among such men, Thomson takes his place; to such men, "The City of Dreadful Night" offers consolation.

"The City of Dreadful Night" is, of course, an important document for the biographer of Thomson.[36] It is the final

---

[36] Its importance as evidence that Thomson used opium has no valid place in this study since neither it nor any other of Thomson's works derives its literary value or philosophic significance from opium dreams. In fact that very question whether Thomson did or did not use opium seems to me of minor importance and completely unanswerable. What little external evidence is available is so contradictory that it must all be considered unreliable: Mrs. Bonner said that Thomson used opium and implied that he took a great deal of it; Salt wrote that there was "some evidence" that he had tried it at one time as an experiment but that "the practice never took a hold on him"; and Foote, who was often with him daily, stated emphatically that Thomson did not use drugs. And the internal evidence is all based on personal interpretation of the poems. Jeannette Marks, the only critic I know to have successfully divorced her considerations from moral aspects, attempted to apply modern psychiatric tests to the problem; but the weakness of her conclusion that Thomson did use opium is that none of the characteristics she cites are symptoms exclusively of drug addiction. They fit acute alcoholism and certain nervous disorders equally well. Thus a positive answer is impossible, but the very fact that the evidence is so slight and so contradictory indicates that if Thomson did take drugs, he did not do so to a great enough extent to make his addiction obvious to everyone.

step in the development of his philosophy, the conclusion at which he arrived after leaving orthodox religion, wandering through a maze of doubts and questionings, struggling in the fruitless search for a compromise. It is the expression of his acceptance of atheism. It is ironic that the comfort of certainty for which he sought so long should in the end have been derived from a negative concept, that the certainty afforded others by Christianity he found in atheism. Having arrived at his belief in atheism and having expressed that belief with all the power at his command, he abandoned philosophic writing almost entirely. Had he never produced another line, the story of his development would still be complete. "The City" is the final chapter.

Because of the importance of "The City" as an expression of Victorian thought, as the statement of Thomson's mature philosophy, and as his greatest work, I offer a cursory survey of the poem, section by section, as well as detailed analyses and criticism of the more significant passages. Such a survey will, in addition to recalling the poem to mind, serve as the basis for my later consideration of the poem as a whole.

The first section describes the City, its geography and its inhabitants. It also offers Thomson's definition of reality:

> For life is but a dream whose shapes return,
>     Some frequently, some seldom, some by night
> And some by day, some night and day: we learn,
>     The while all change and many vanish quite,
> In their recurrence with recurrent changes
> A certain seeming order; where this ranges
>     We count things real. . . .

Such, the order of recurrent dreams, is the reality of the City.[37]

The second section, whose theme is the purposelessness of life, is marked by a figure of speech at once striking and perfect, a figure which produces a visual image that contributes a dramatic quality to the thought. Questioned concerning his unceasing pilgrimages to three shrines, the cathedral where died Faith, the villa where died Love, and the squalid hovel where died Hope, a man likens his life to the mechanism of a clock which, though rendered meaningless by the loss of hands and dial, continues to function.

> The works proceed until run down; although
> Bereft of purpose, void of use, still go.

The following section, iii, tells of eyes that are able to see figures in the darkness of the City and of ears that make out sounds in the silence.

The desert scene, section iv, is the most spectacular of the whole poem, the first to catch the attention of the casual reader and longest to be remembered. The first half of the section, describing the speaker's journey through the desert, resembles a Dürer woodblock of the Apocrypha, filled with strange, horrible, fantastic shapes and scenes—a dragon with eyes of fire, sharp claws, swift talons; a hillock burning with a myriad of flame-points; a Sabbath of Serpents, writhing and hissing; meteors in the blank black sky; the zenith a gulf of flame.

---

[37] In his *Etudes de psychologie littéraire,* which includes the finest analysis of "The City" I have ever found, Louis Cazamian wrote: "Ainsi la Cité de la Nuit existe dans nos coeurs; c'est la capitale funèbre des tristesses, le centre où convergent nos rêveries amères découragées; et sur nos visions fugitives et persistantes, se construit l'universalité de son empire" (p. 231).

But it has a vividness not found in Dürer, gained by the use of color and especially by an even greater sense of the dynamic than that artist was able to achieve; it is all alive and moving; even the sky and earth are like powerful, evil monsters about to close in on the traveler. In the second half of the section the wayfarer meets, in this scene of horror, a woman carrying her burning heart in her hand as a lantern—Matilda. She takes with her, when she parts from him, his better half, leaving only the worse alive on earth. The act is symbolic of what Thomson conceived to be the difference between past possibility and present reality, between what might have been had Matilda lived and what actually was.

This striking material Thomson handled with great skill. The descriptions are so clear and vivid that the reader not only sees the scenes but also feels the thick air clotting in his throat and the carnivorous breath hot upon him. The trancelike mood of eerie unreality is quickly established and consistently maintained. But most effective is Thomson's use of the line-and-a-half-long refrain with which he opens each stanza,

> As I came through the desert thus it was,
> As I came through the desert . . .

together with the short-line refrain which closes the first six of the eleven stanzas,

> . . . I strode on austere;
> No hope could have no fear.[38]

---

[38] The last line is unquestionably inspired by Leopardi. Prior to the writing of even the first of "The City" Thomson had translated a line from one of Leopardi's letters thus: "Where is no hope is no place for inquietude."

The two last lines of the remaining five stanzas follow the same metrical pattern and use the same rhyme. This unusual refrain device affords the monotony which contributes to the almost hypnotic effect of the section and at the same time to the nervous stimulation which gives it its excitement, like the long roll of drums.

The danger inherent in the use of the autobiographical elements, for without subtle handling they would have introduced a foreign note and broken the mood of the whole, Thomson avoided by dissolving them so completely in the phantasy that they add to rather than detract from the total effect.

Section v is concerned with the impossibility of escape from the City—

> . . . who once hath paced that dolent city
> Shall pace it often . . .

—and reminds one of Thomson's unsuccessful efforts to escape it. Section vi presents a conversation between two men who had sought entrance to hell; because they had had no hope to offer at its portals as fees of admission, hell was closed to them. And section vii deals with the phantoms of the City.

The dialogue, section viii, is one of the three most important parts of the poem, biographically, philosophically, and artistically. The two speakers represent the two reactions which Thomson himself felt towards the world: the one, emotional, bitterly resentful; the other, cold, resigned, unflinchingly logical. The emotional speaker laments that he is denied even the simplest desires of man—food, health, sleep. Then, as his bitterness grows, he curses God:

". . . yet I would rather be
My miserable self than He, than He
Who formed such creatures to his own disgrace.

"The vilest thing must be less vile than Thou
From whom it had its being, God and Lord!"

The logical speaker replies that there is no Being, God or
Fiend, at once so wicked, foolish, and insane as to produce
man.

"The world rolls round for ever like a mill;
It grinds out death and life and good and ill;
It has no purpose, heart or mind or will.

.    .    .

"Man might know one thing were his sight less dim;
That it whirls not to suit his petty whim,
That it is quite indifferent to him."

He concludes his cold, deterministic answers with a bit of
comfort:

"Nay, does it treat him harshly as he saith?
It grinds him some slow years of bitter breath,
Then grinds him back into eternal death."

This section exhibits the excellences of writing of which
Thomson was capable at his best. His poetic treatment of
subject is marked by artistic simplicity: the style is straightforward and unlabored; the diction is so natural that it ap-
proaches the colloquial in places; and the uncomplicated
metrical form, iambic pentameter triplets, is suited to the
subject and mood. The dramatic treatment, that of casting
the material into the form of a dialogue and setting the two

speakers in opposition to each other, is no less effective. But most striking is the harsh restraint imposed on the intense emotion. The lament of the first speaker is gently ridiculed by the logical reply of the second; the impassioned rush of words with which the former curses God is calmly checked by the slow, dry speech of the latter. By such a method of stern control, Thomson gave the impression of frustration and in so doing deepened the passion. Thus he gave to this section a roughness and a strength which makes it unforgettable.

The following section, ix, describes the sight and sound of a huge wagon, pulled by straining horses. The speculation that perhaps its load is the joy, the peace, the hope, "the abortions of all things good [that] have been strangled by that City's curse" is poignantly applicable to Thomson's own life in London.

The mansion scene, section x, is one of the poorest of the poem. In each room of the mansion, hung with funereal black, is a picture or an image of a young girl, and in the last room is a man, praying by the side of a bier on which is the body of the girl. His prayer begins:

> The chambers of the mansion of my heart,
> In every one whereof thine image dwells,
> Are black with grief eternal for thy sake.

The autobiographical intent of the section is clear: the man is Thomson and the girl Matilda.

One of the weaknesses of the section is its romantic sentimentalism, which has already been observed both in Thomson's life, as in his use of the name Vanolis, and in his work, as in portions of "Vane's Story." Another, springing directly from the first, is that the man at the side of the bier is individualized, is James Thomson, whose fiancée has died, whereas the concept of "The City" as a whole calls for generalized figures standing for whole groups of men. And in all other instances, with the exception of the desert scene, the characters of "The City" do have general significance. The desert scene, in which Thomson and Matilda also appear as individuals, is saved from similar failure because it had a dominant mood of general appeal to which the characters are subordinated. The mansion scene, however, has no such mood to save it and it therefore strikes a discordant note.

Section xi tells what sort of men live in the City, men like Thomson who

> . . . pierce life's pleasant veil of various error
> To reach that void of darkness and old terror
>    Wherein expire the lamps of hope and faith?

In the following section, xii, a heterogeneous collection of people—kings, writers, clowns, judges, drunkards—are shown entering a cathedral. As each passes the door, he gives the password, telling what he has been and whence he came, ending his confession with the phrase, "I wake from day-dreams to this real night."

Section xiii deals with a subject which Thomson had often touched briefly in both prose and poetry: the folly of man who, though he wastes in "dread undelight" his life on earth, yet moans that time is fleeting and asks therefore the boon of immortality. The wiser inhabitants of the City do not ask for immortality, for a longer term of strife, but only for "speedy death in full fruition."

The cathedral scene, section xiv, the second of the most important parts of the poem, is the statement in dramatic form of Thomson's mature philosophy, his only complete expression of it. As I have pointed out, he had been seeking certainty for almost two decades, examining and rejecting various religions and philosophies. Early in the section he writes:

> . . . I have searched the highths and depths, the scope
> Of all our universe, with desperate hope
>   To find some solace for your wild unrest.

And at the same time he had been gradually building up his own philosophy, especially in "The Doom of a City" and "A Lady of Sorrow." By the time he wrote "The City" he was ready to enunciate it: "And now at last authentic word I bring."

The scene is laid in a cathedral. The members of the City, of the dolorous brotherhood, stand each by himself in the fane, silent with the apathy of despair. There is no organ strain, no murmur of whispered prayer, no chant, no clinking of censer. Then from the pulpit comes the voice of the priest like a peal in midnight quiet:

> Good tidings of great joy for you, for all:
> There is no God. . . .

The simple statement, without preamble or introduction, without reservation or modification, couched ironically in the phraseology of the old Christmas hymn, is startlingly dramatic. The priest continues in his quiet, straightforward manner. "The Person," conscious and omnipotent, whom men curse for having created them and then curse again for endowing them with immortal life that can never be relinquished

[ 105 ]

even in the tomb, is but a dark delusion of a dream. "There is no God."

And there is yet more comfort:

> This little life is all we must endure,
> The grave's most holy peace is ever sure.

What mortality there is is not of the individual soul, but of the material elements of which man's body is composed. His flesh dissolves to merge afresh in earth, air, water, plants, and other men; his soul, his conscious individuality, dies once and for all, assured of oblivion. He is not condemned to live on after death.

Nor is man the apex of the animal world. His supremacy will end when a higher species of animal develops to displace him as he in the past displaced a lower order. Man is no more enduring than the mammoth, for the universe is ordered in accordance with the supreme and immutable laws of nature—unconscious laws, which have no special clause "of cruelty or kindness, love or hate" for man. Man, toad, vulture—all creatures are born, live, and die by these laws:

> If one is born a certain day on earth,
> All times and forces tended to that birth,
> Nor all the world could change or hinder it.

There is in the universe no good nor ill, no blessing nor curse—only Necessity: "I find alone Necessity Supreme."

The priest ends his discourse by repeating his assurance of mortality, which frees men from the dread of an afterlife.

> Lo, you are free to end it when you will,
> Without the fear of waking after death.—
> . . . "End it when you will."

This, then, is Thomson's statement of his philosophy, and as such the section is the heart not only of "The City" but of all his writings. It is no exaggeration to say that in many respects it is the most significant piece of work he ever did.

But the cathedral scene is memorable not alone for its importance in the history of Thomson's thought, but also for its beauty. Thomson always wrote best when he felt most strongly, when the intellectual concept he was attempting to express was pregnant with emotion. Here the concept is clear; the treatment is simple and lucid, unclouded by rhetoric or trite poetic diction; and the emotion is intense, lifting the thought above mere philosophic versification and transmuting it into high poetry. The section is marked also, as are other shorter passages in Thomson's writing, by rich, smooth, flowing music. Yet it is not mellifluous nor cloying. When writing at his best, Thomson recognized fully the value of the commonplace word and the rough or irregular line. He recognized too the dramatic effectiveness of the simple construction. This cathedral scene is, in my opinion, his greatest poetic achievement.

The following section, xv, acting both as an interlude between the message of the priest and the reaction of his audience and as a means of relief after the intensity of the cathedral scene, deals with the idea that men grouped together mutually affect each other, that each breathes his life out into the air to be breathed in again by his fellow creatures. In the City, his breath is an infection of sadness and despair: "Each adding poison to the poisoned air."

Section xvi returns to the cathedral. A few minutes of silence follow the priest's message; then suddenly a man's knife-edged voice cuts the air, quiet and restrained at first but growing shriller and shriller as the passion of rebellious despair mounts within him. The priest is right, he laments. No personal life exists beyond the grave. He has had but one chance in all eternity, one brief lifetime to taste the joys of living, intellectual and social pleasures, a home with wife and children, the delights of art and nature, health, and serene old age. Yet none of these simple things, the "sublime prerogatives of Man," has he known—none nor any part of one:

> This chance was never offered me before;
>
> .　　　.　　　.
>
> This chance recurreth never, nevermore;
>
> 　　　　.　　　.　　　.
>
> And this sole chance was frustrate from my birth.

In this section, as in the dialogue, section viii, which it strongly resembles despite the shift of emphasis from the intellectual concept to the emotional reaction, it is Thomson himself speaking from his own experience, enumerating those simple desires, the fulfillment of which free man has always regarded, theoretically at least, as his right. Rebelling against the assurance of mortality which destroys every hope of future life, he passionately demands at least some of those few things which make for a happy life. In his despair he cries out, "Our life's a cheat, our death a black abyss." But the answer of the priest is inexorable:

> This life itself holds nothing good for us,
> But it ends soon and nevermore can be.

In the section on the stars, xvii, Thomson seeks to replace the romantic fallacy that "the heavens respond" to what man feels with the scientific concept of a mechanistic universe. In lines of lyric beauty he describes the shimmering light of the stars, transforming dewy grass to faery lakes, striking on quivering water and crystallike windows. So alive the stars seem that man finds emotion in them as though they were conscious, vital beings:

> With such a living light these dead eyes shine,
>    These eyes of sightless heaven, that as we gaze
> We read a pity, tremulous, divine,
>    Or cold majestic scorn in their pure rays:

Then he looks at them less romantically. They are but cold, ineffectual whorls of matter spinning mechanically, each in its determined orbit, in limitless space; and

> The spheres eternal are a grand illusion,
> The empyréan is a void abyss.

The contrast between the two concepts is handled quietly and with restraint. As a result, a mood of loneliness and loss and a feeling of almost frightening insignificance, the unstated themes of the section, are established.

In the following section, xviii, Thomson turns from the beauty of the stars to paint an ugly, sordid picture of a man driven insane by despair. Crawling animallike, with an animallike expression on his face, he would escape from the City by tracing his way back along the paths of life to infancy or even to the womb. But this is no escape, for were he to accomplish his purpose, a whole long lifetime would again stretch out before him. Truly he is mad. If he will but wait, death will shortly rescue him forever.

And death is near by, for through the City flows the river

of suicides. The section describing the river, xix, ends with the explanation of why all the inhabitants do not cut short their unhappy lives by self-destruction. Some do not because of a vague, unformed curiosity to see

> . . . what shifts are yet in the dull play
> For our illusion. . . .

Others refrain because it seems not worth the grief they would cause "dear foolish friends." Still others fail to act because of apathy, which makes even suicide seem too much trouble since life is

> . . . but for one night after all:
> What matters one brief night of dreary pain?

There is no hint of which of these explanations answers the oft-repeated query, why did not Thomson commit suicide? It is my belief, however, based on no more substantial evidence than his character, that he was one of those with curiosity.

Section xx, the last of the three most significant of the poem, may be called the history of man. In front of a cathedral are two stone figures facing each other: a couchant sphinx, symbolic of the immutable, unconscious laws of nature; and an angel with hands on the cross hilt of a naked sword as though about to strike, symbolic of religious man. The angel believes his religion a dynamic power by which he can control nature. There is a loud crash—the wings of the angel have fallen; religion has proved impotent against the sphinx. The angel has now become a warrior, leaning on his sword, feeling himself self-sufficient. He is confident that he can conquer without the aid of a god. Science and philosophy are his new weapons, giving him strength as great as religious faith. Then another sudden clatter—and the warrior's sword lies broken at his feet. An unarmed, suppliant man remains, helpless, hopeless, despairing, casting himself on the mercy of nature. But yet another crash is heard. Man is destroyed and his shattered figure lies between the great unfeeling paws of the sphinx. The moon moves on its course. The universe is unconscious of the annihilation of man.

In this powerful section Thomson, by means of symbolism, has expressed in eight short stanzas the history of nineteen centuries of thought. Yet he has not overloaded his writing; there is nothing complex or abstruse about it. The symbolism is clear and he has resisted the temptation to expand his theme or follow its ramifications. Yet by his carefully drawn figures and by definite, significant action, he suggests all that he has not written and stimulates the reader to supply that which he has omitted.

The final section of the poem, xxi, though of less importance than the preceding, is nevertheless very effective and justly famous. The first half introduces the great bronze statue which looks out over the City from the bleak and bare uplands to the north. Explaining that it is the central figure of Albrecht Dürer's "Melencholia," Thomson describes that print in detail. The central figure is a large, winged woman. Seated, she supports her head on her clenched fist and peers unseeingly into space, her gaze rebellious, intense, despairing. She wears the garb of a housewife, a bunch of keys hanging at her waist. In her lap are a book and a pair of compasses; at her feet, the tools of carpentry, a censer, and a crystal ball. Among these lies a sleeping wolfhound.[39] Above her hang scales, an hourglass, and a magic square.

---

[39] The line describing the wolfhound reads, "With the keen wolfhound sleeping undistraught." The line as Thomson originally intended it was, "With the poor creature for dissection brought." He had con-

# JAMES THOMSON (B.V.)

The second half of the section is Thomson's interpretation of the print. Melencholia, weary, sick of soul, works doggedly with the instruments of science, of building, of religion, of magic, always to be defeated in her quest for the answer of the meaning of the universe and the things therein. None of man's tools of brain or hand has helped her; she is no nearer understanding of the world than she was before these were invented. They have all proved impotent. In her eyes one reads why all her efforts have been useless, her labors futile.

> The sense that every struggle brings defeat
>     Because Fate holds no prize to crown success;
> That all the oracles are dumb or cheat
>     Because they have no secret to express;
> That none can pierce the vast black veil uncertain
> Because there is no light beyond the curtain;
>     That all is vanity and nothingness.

Such is the figure that overlooks the City. To it the inhabitants look up,

> The strong to drink new strength of iron endurance,
> The weak new terrors; all, renewed assurance
>     And confirmation of the old despair.

---

sidered the animal a dead sheep brought for anatomical study; but observing that Ruskin called it a wolf or wolfhound, he wrote William M. Rossetti to ask his opinion. Rossetti apparently concurred with Ruskin, for Thomson changed the line, calling it "a villainous makeshift." Because the original line and interpretation are better than the revised, I should like to agree that the animal is a dead sheep; but I admit that I cannot believe it such, especially after examining "Le Cellule de St. Jerome," which Dürer did in the same year as the "Melencholia," 1514, in which an animal, very similar in general outline to the one in question, is clearly a dog. The two prints have enough in common to influence one to believe that Dürer intended both animals as dogs.

So closes "The City of Dreadful Night" on the note which has run throughout the poem like the low moan of a bass viol, dull despair.

In examining "The City" section by section, I have indicated the literary characteristics and merits of the more important individual units. The poem as a whole naturally shows qualities that are not apparent in the parts. Of these the first is the sustention of a single mood throughout a long poem; the dominant feeling, compounded of despair and hopelessness and futility and weariness, never breaks for a moment. With consummate artistry Thomson created and held this mood by the expression and re-expression of its source: the quiet, sincere, unchanging conviction that the laws of the universe are unconscious of man, immutable by him, and supreme over him, and that he is powerless, therefore, to do more than await the oblivion of merciful death. This mood, with its overtone of bitterness, Thomson has given great variation by reiterating it in varied forms and language, by showing it in its diverse aspects. The curse uttered by the first speaker in the dialogue scene is a cry wrung from him by despair; the discourse of the priest in the cathedral is a leaden statement of despair; Melencholia overlooking the City is a picture of despair. Like the composer of a symphony Thomson, after establishing his theme, worked it out in different keys with different instruments. The achievement of such sustention of mood is the more remarkable when one remembers that the poem was started in 1870, laid aside for three years, and finally finished in 1874. Thus one recognizes that the sustention is the result of genius, of painstaking craftsmanship, and of careful labor.

The structure of the poem constitutes its second major excellence. By a tight, firm structure Thomson was able to attain his unity of mood and of composition and at the same time to achieve great variety. The work is made up of two threads, appearing in alternate sections, each marked by its stanzaic peculiarity and by its proper subject matter. The Proem and odd-numbered sections are written in seven-line stanzas, rhyming *ababccb;* the even-numbered sections are either introduced by or entirely written in six-line stanzas rhyming *ababcc.* Those in which only the first few stanzas are so written conclude with different stanzaic forms, which are usually short.[40] The even-numbered sections are episodic in character, quoting the words of one or two speakers or telling of an incident. They give action, or the impression of action, to the poem and relieve the meditative quality of the whole although they actually present different aspects of the thought. The odd-numbered sections are more purely speculative or reflective, offering generalizations, descriptions, moods, etc. As is apparent, the structure is mechanical and as such carries the danger of dominating the poet. But Thomson, far from being mastered by the form, is so much the master of it that it never intrudes. Indeed, even a careful reader is usually unaware of it.

It is the episodic sections that give the poem its third noteworthy characteristic, a strong dramatic quality. Each with its own background, characters, and action (expressed or implied), the episodes permit a greater variety and stimulate

---

[40] Such are section iv, the body of which is written in a five-line stanza rhyming *abbccdd,* with a two-line refrain, *ee;* section vi, with a three-line stanza rhyming *aaa;* section viii, with a four-line stanza, *abba;* section x, with an unrhymed three-line stanza; section xii, with a four-line stanza of *aabb;* and section xvi, with a four-line stanza of *abab.*

a more intense emotion than would purely expository writing on the same theme. They show not merely an abstract idea but also the relation of the individual man to that idea, as in the second cathedral scene, wherein the bitterly resentful speaker, angry with disappointment, protests against the assurance that there is no afterlife and the priest finds comfort in the certainty that this little life is all he must endure. These characters live. The reader understands and sympathizes with them, even shares their reactions. Accordingly, these dramatic scenes move him with the force of intimate human experience.

The dramatic quality of the episodes is heightened by several literary devices. Thomson was well aware of the value of contrasts, contrasts between reactions, as those of the rebel and the priest; between characters, as the emotional first speaker in the dialogue and the impassive, intellectual second speaker; between images evoked, as the beauties of the star-filled sky and the ugly picture, in the following section, of the animallike madman. He also knew when to check intense emotion momentarily, when to afford his reader relief, as in the interlude between the two cathedral scenes. But most important, he recognized the dramatic quality of restraint. The discourse of the priest in the cathedral scene, perhaps the most intense passage in the whole work, is low-voiced and quiet. The sphinx scene, with its themes of frustration and impotence, is so controlled that it is almost cold. Thus has Thomson made the mood of despair dramatic and beautiful.

Critics of Thomson's day, and many since, have asked why he wrote "The City of Dreadful Night." The answers he stated clearly in the Proem. In the first place it was for his personal satisfaction.

Because a cold rage seizes one at whiles
   To show the bitter old and wrinkled truth
Stripped naked of all vesture that beguiles,
   False dreams, false hopes, false masks and modes of youth;
Because it gives some sense of power and passion
In helpless impotence to try to fashion
   Our woe in living words howe'er uncouth.

Surely the feeling of power which accompanies expression, however futile and illogical, is an adequate reason for writing. To such a man as Thomson, who had no other vent for his emotions, no other activity for his mind and body, writing brought release and satisfaction.

The second answer is less personal but quite as sincere. Thomson was, as I have noted, a deeply sympathetic man, one who felt the sorrows of his fellow men. He desired, therefore, to alleviate their suffering. He saw but one way of accomplishing this end: to afford them whatever intellectual and emotional comfort there was to be derived from the realization that they were not alone in their anguish, that the members of the dolorous fraternity were many.[41]

And he succeeded in offering solace to those members, succeeded as no other writer I know; but not, I think, in the way he intended, for there is but little consolation in knowing oneself a member of the sad brotherhood. Rather, Thomson comforted by expressing the unexpressed, afforded relief by making articulate that which lies inarticulate in the members of the City. They read the poem, and in the reading they find

---

[41] In "Open Secret Societies," 1865, he wrote, "Though no word of mine will ever convert anyone from being himself into another me, my word may bring cheer and comfort and self-knowledge to others who are more or less like myself, and who may have thought themselves peculiar and outcast."

comfort and release and strength in the beautiful expression of their own unrest and pain. It is for them a catharsis. They see in the poem not Thomson's ideas, not Thomson's emotions, but their own hidden, uneasy thoughts and feelings. Thus "The City" is a personal poem to those who understand and feel it. But there are many for whom "The City of Dreadful Night" has no appeal, who fail to understand why it has deep significance for others. Of them Thomson wrote in the Proem.

> Surely I write not for the hopeful young,
>     Or those who deem their happiness of worth,
> Or such as pasture and grow fat among
>     The shows of life and feel nor doubt nor dearth,
> Or pious spirits with a God above them
> To sanctify and glorify and love them,
>     Or sages who foresee a heaven on earth.
>
> For none of these I write, and none of these
>     Could read the writing if they deigned to try.

They may scan the words of "The City," but they are emotionally incapable of understanding the meaning.

# CHAPTER IV

# In the Room

## 1874-1881

THOMSON'S story from the beginning of 1874 to October, 1881, is best told by his diaries.[1] These little green clothbound books, mere records of daily routine, of finances, of letters received and answered, make poignant reading despite their unemotional, factual character, for they tell of a life which would have been pitiful were it not marked by sober pride and quiet dignity. These eight long years were ones of humiliating poverty, steadily deteriorating health, thwarted hopes, misfortunes, and failures.

Not even the publication of "The City of Dreadful Night" in the first half of 1874 was such as to give Thomson any sense of satisfaction. "The City," which he fully recognized as his greatest work, he saw appear in small, badly set, blurred type on the cheap, rough paper of the *National Reformer,* divided arbitrarily into four installments to fit the needs for copy.[2]

---

[1] These seven diaries (that of 1875 has been either destroyed or lost) are all in the possession of Percy Dobell, who generously allowed me to use them.

[2] March 22, April 12 and 26, and May 17, 1874.

Nor had he hope that, coming out in such a periodical, it would receive wide attention or an unprejudiced hearing.[3] It is little wonder, then, that the diary entries concerning its publication were very brief and savored more of frustration than of pleasure.[4]

It was during the publication of "The City" that Thomson suffered the loss of his closest, most sympathetic friend, Austin Holyoake. The quality of Thomson's emotions is indicated by the careful restraint of his diary entry of April 10, noting only that Holyoake had died shortly after one o'clock, and by the cruel accuracy of a second entry, five days later: "Saw Austin—still looking better than I have lately seen him sometimes in life—jaw fallen, right eye a little open, leg a skeleton from the large knee-bone." Here is Thomson's grief coupled with his characteristic dislike of a show of emotion.[5]

Still other disappointments were in store for him during

---

[3] As a matter of fact it did attract sufficient attention to receive notices in both the *Spectator* and the *Academy,* and George Meredith saw it in the *National Reformer.*

[4] Thomson was well aware of the reputation of the *National Reformer.* He had written in "Bumble, Bumbledon, and Bumbleist," as has been noted above, that it was "a periodical of deepest disrepute." He had commented in a letter to William M. Rossetti that his only production "in reputable society" was "Sunday up the River," which had appeared in *Fraser's Magazine.* And he had doubted that James Anthony Froude would welcome him into his home when his connection with the *National Reformer* became known.

[5] In his diary of April 16, 1874, Thomson wrote that he had sketched and rewritten the description of Holyoake's funeral for the *National Reformer,* "as quiet and simple as I could well make it." This stands in contrast to an entry of February 22, 1879: "In today's *Athenaeum:* O'Shaughnessy, a poem, *In Memoriam,* of his wife, who died on the 8th inst., just a fortnight back; or rather in proclamation of his soundless, bottomless, endless grief."

1874. Bertram Dobell, a rare-book dealer and scholar, proposed to publish a volume of Thomson's verse. Although he fully recognized the difficulties surrounding such an enterprise, Thomson was heartened by the fact that a man of Dobell's standing thought so well of his writings, and for several months the two worked and schemed together. But the cost of publication, they discovered, would be great; and Dobell, sincerely as he tried, was unable just then to raise money to meet the expense of a project which, as Thomson remarked, was as likely to fail as to succeed.[6] Thus what little hope he had entertained and the dreams he had enjoyed vanished.

Throughout these years Thomson's dipsomania was steadily growing worse. From 1876 on, the breaks in the diaries, probably indicating attacks, become longer with each occurrence. An interval of abstinence and hard work, when all went well and he wrote rapidly, was followed by a fit of despondency. Day by day his depression became more insupportable until in reckless desperation he surrendered himself to the relief he found in alcohol. During the attacks, lasting from a few days during the early part of this period to two or three weeks as his health gave way under them, he was entirely irresponsible. He remembered little or nothing of his actions when they were past,[7] and returning to sanity was filled with disgust and self-abhorrence.[8] But not once in the seven volumes of the diaries does he mention these attacks; indeed, there is not so much as an identifiable circumlocution. Such a lack of comment, even in the privacy of his diaries, indicates his attitude toward his dipsomania and gives further weight

<hr/>

[6] Salt, *op. cit.,* pp. 117–118.
[7] G. W. Foote, "James Thomson. I. The Man," *Progress,* April, 1884.
[8] J. W. Barrs, quoted by Salt, 1914 edition, p. 107.

to the assertions of Salt and Dobell that he never ceased to fight against it.

Thomson's actions while suffering an attack, his death, and the sensational stories written about it have given the impression that his mode of life was, from the nature of his character, irregular. The contrary is true. Thomson was by nature more orderly and methodical than the average person, as almost every page of the diaries proves. The very small form of the entries is symbolic. In the top corner, in very small writing, was a note on the weather. Then came the account of the day divided into "Morng.," "Aftn.," and "Evg." Every letter received or written was noted and usually the contents summarized. Material sent to the editor, proof sheets received or returned, and pay received were all listed. He noted every person he saw in the course of the day and frequently the subjects of conversation. In the lower left hand corner was the last item: how many skuttles of coal he had used during the day and how full each was. Moreover, his activities varied from day to day almost as little as the form of the entries. In such manner Thomson conducted himself normally; it was only during the attacks of dipsomania that his life was irregular.

In addition to the dipsomania, and probably because of it, Thomson suffered insomnia. In his diary he noted on October 19, 1877, "For the past fortnight my old friend Insomnia has been with me." The complaint was not new, however; he advised his sister-in-law not to read "The City," "In the Room," and "To Our Ladies of Death," because they had been "written under the evil inspiration of the Melancholy of Insomnia." [9] But because of his failing health it was more

---

[9] Diary, April 9, 1880.

serious than it had been earlier. In the poem "Insomnia," he left a picture of the long sleepless nights when he lay tortured by his taut nerves and intense imagination. The room was filled with huge, shadowy forms that oppressed him, and time stretched out endlessly as his heart pounded till it seemed that his body could no longer stand it. Although he passed over the subject in the diaries with but brief references, this powerful description of his suffering permits some understanding of the curse that was Thomson's insomnia.

After the sunstroke in Spain, Thomson never fully regained his health. Scattered throughout his diaries are entries concerned with indigestion, biliousness, diarrhea, and passing blood,[10] constriction of the chest over and above the heart and rheumatic pains in the shoulder and arms, which made him remember his father's paralytic stroke,[11] frequent and long-lasting colds in the chest and throat.[12] The stomach and intestinal troubles were no doubt caused at least in part by alcohol, but he seems to have been unaware of the relationship, for he attempted to cure them by fasting and purging with castor oil.[13] And constriction about the heart is a common symptom of alcoholism. The frequency and tenacity of the colds gives evidence of his general physical condition and low resistance. That his nerves were also affected, probably by his drinking, is indicated by other diary entries, such as the one for August 14, 1879, in which he complained of excessive

---

[10] See, for example, January 31, February 1-2, 1876; June 5, June 18-19, 1878; January 26-31, March 7, November 14-17, 1879; September 12, 1881; etc.

[11] See especially February 10-28, 1879.

[12] October 27, 1876; April 15-20, 1878; December 27, 1879; April 5-12, 1880; January 23, September 12, 1881; etc.

[13] October 15, 1874; November 15-16, 1879; etc.

itching, "here, there, and everywhere though uninfested by bugs or fleas, and though my skin is quite clean," for he bathed every morning. A dose of bromide might have afforded him the relief which bathing failed to give. It is possible that the often-mentioned drowsiness which forced him to spend many afternoons dozing instead of walking was also due in part to nervous exhaustion, though it may have been simply the result of his insomnia.[14]

Visual evidence of Thomson's physical decline may be found in his handwriting. In 1874 it was small and firm and neat, but year by year it grew increasingly large and shaky. The lines, at first straight and true, lost their strength and tended to be crooked. The early legible script gave way to a scrawl at times almost unreadable. By 1881 it was feeble and laborious, like that of an old man, or a young child who carefully draws the characters. Powerfully it shows the debility which had overcome Thomson.

To give his aching body and frayed nerves a rest was, however, impossible. Even when he was most miserable his need for money sufficient to obtain food and lodgings kept him at his table in the British Museum or in his quarters. He continued to contribute to the *National Reformer* until July, 1875, when he left Bradlaugh's employ. A few months later he started writing for *Cope's Tobacco Plant,* a monthly magazine which, until it ceased publication in January, 1881, was his steadiest and best market. In addition he wrote for *The Secularist,* a weekly founded in January, 1876, by G. W. Foote and G. J. Holyoake, a brother of Austin, in opposition to Bradlaugh, whose highhandedness was causing dissension

---

[14] May 27, June 19, 1876; February 17, March 7, 1879; etc.

within the Secular Society. To it alone he gave seventy-one items in its first twelve months, a greater number than he had contributed in any earlier year, even to the *National Reformer*. *The Secularist* failed after but a year and a half,[15] but it was succeeded in January, 1879, by *The Liberal*, started by G. W. Foote, and to it also Thomson contributed. In a single typical month, April, 1876, he was working on the four Rabelais articles for *Cope's*, and for *The Secularist* he was writing "Mr. Matthew Arnold on the Church of England," "The Worth of Metaphysical Systems," "The System of Spinoza," and a series of six articles that made up a biographical sketch of Heine. All except the "Mr. Matthew Arnold" entailed much reading and studying. And for his own pleasure Thomson spent odd hours translating Leopardi.[16]

Despite such productivity Thomson was hard pressed for money. John Fraser, editor of *Cope's*, took all that Thomson sent him and paid punctually and as liberally as he could; but Thomson's arrangement with *The Secularist* was that until the editors should get their new venture firmly established financially he would receive no pay. Unfortunately the time to pay back debts never arrived and the career of *The Secularist* ended without Thomson's having received a penny. With the subsequent *Liberal* he made a more businesslike arrangement, but it was not satisfactorily carried out; pay was so slow that he eventually quarreled bitterly with the editor on the subject. Thus he frequently was without adequate funds. In March, 1876, after he had been ill as the

---

[15] Accurately speaking, *The Secularist* did not fail but rather merged, in 1877, with the *Secular Review*. Thomson did not continue on the staff after the merger.

[16] Diary, April, 1876.

result of an accident,[17] he wrote Fraser, asking for an advance of a few pounds.[18] In December of that year he received twelve pounds twelve shillings for the first three parts of the Ben Jonson study and the same day turned the twelve pounds over to his housekeeper and landlord, reserving but only the twelve shillings for himself.[19] By October, 1879, he had sold some of his books "when hard up." [20] In June, 1880, another request to Fraser brought the desired ten pounds with a note that he might have more if he wished. To the diary entry telling of this offer he added the single word, "Yes!" [21] Again in October of the same year he found it necessary to ask Fraser for an advance. In a note of thanks showing that he still retained his pride, he remarked that, although hard pressed, he did not wish to impose and if Fraser needed the money for more urgent business, he could get along without it.[22] It may be noted in passing that Fraser's consistent willingness to advance Thomson money is good evidence of the

---

[17] Salt, *op. cit.,* p. 142, wrote only of a serious fall which Thomson suffered, but gave no details. The diary entry of February 29, 1876, is as follows: "X Accident X Doctor." The word "doctor" is repeated, without amplification, in the entries of March 1, 2, 4, and 6. Again for November 9, the same year, there is the entry, "X Accident X." The entries of the following days, November 10 through 15, indicate that he stayed at home the entire time. The entries of February 29 and November 9 are the only ones mentioning any accident. It would be dangerous to assume that the word *accident* is a circumlocution for an attack of dipsomania, especially since it occurs only twice; more reasonable is the suggestion that Thomson suffered some minor accident during an attack. This is strengthened by Salt's method of handling the subject, which has a tone of circumspection rather than ignorance of facts.

[18] Diary, March 8, 1876.

[19] Diary, December 22, 1876.

[20] Letter of October 19, 1879, quoted by Salt, *op. cit.,* p. 138.

[21] Diary, June 28, 1880.

[22] Diary, October 10, 1880.

fact that at so late a date as 1880 he considered him a responsible man who could be trusted to turn in the copy for which
he had received pay. The diaries abound in evidence of Thomson's poverty, but there is no hint whatsoever that he ever
begged or asked for a loan he did not expect to be able to
repay.[23]

Seeing no hope of improving the situation by his writing,
Thomson thought again in 1875 of the possibility of publishing a volume of poems. Refusing Dobell's suggestion of
financing by subscription, he started to search for a publisher.
He had little hope of obtaining cash, but he felt that by publishing he might gain a reputation which would enable him to
place his work with better paying periodicals.[24] In October,
1876, he took his manuscript to Messrs. King and Co., who
kept it for four months before requesting Thomson to with-
draw it.[25] He next took it to Chatto and Windus, with the
suggestion that they publish it on commission, but again he
met with failure.[26] In June, 1877, he wrote Dobell that he had
found it hopeless to attempt publication before winter.[27] In
February, 1878, Trübners put him off till the following
June.[28] And so it went. Thomson understood the attitude of

---

[23] Another, but unverified, story of Thomson's poverty comes from
Hypatia Bradlaugh Bonner, who reported that a member of the Bradlaugh family found a silver tankard belonging to Thomson in a pawn-
shop, redeemed it, and sent it back to him. In his diary Thomson wrote
on June 19, 1879, "Trouselle handed me an old silver tankard (which
I left with poor Mrs. B.) and a note from Alice." Which story is true
(indeed, both may be) cannot at this time be determined.

[24] Letter to Dobell, July 9, 1875, quoted by Salt, *op. cit.,* p. 126.

[25] Diary, February 22, 1877.

[26] Diary, February 27, 1877.

[27] Letter to Dobell, June 22, 1877, quoted by Salt, *op. cit.,* p. 134.

[28] Letter to Dobell, February 12, 1878, quoted by Dobell in *The
Laureate of Pessimism,* p. 31.

the publishers; he wrote, "Verse by an unknown man is always a drug on the market, and, when it is Atheistic, it is a virulently poisonous drug with which respectable publishers would rather have nothing to do." [29] But he could hardly excuse those who promised, delayed, and then repudiated their promises.

Thomson's life was further embittered during this period by the severance of two friendships. In 1875 he broke completely with his friend of twenty-four years, Charles Bradlaugh. Letters to Bertram Dobell show a growing resentment during the first six months of the year and complain that he was being crowded off the *National Reformer* by Bradlaugh and Annie Besant, a newcomer writing over the name "Ajax," and that his anonymity had not been respected. In July came the break. Of it Thomson wrote only briefly: "I am quite off this now, B. having taken the first opportunity of terminating our connection, which I myself had only submitted to for sometime past because it afforded me mere subsistence." Later, however, he remarked that he had not cared "to be gagged at the pleasure of Mr. B." [30] Any possibility of healing the breach was eliminated by Thomson's subsequent efforts to collect a sum of money due him for work for the *National Reformer*. In view of Bradlaugh's undeniable kindnesses and

---

[29] Facsimile of one page of a letter from Thomson to "one of the editors," otherwise unidentified, included in the Leek Bijou reprint of *The Story of a Famous Old Jewish Firm and Other Pieces in Prose and Rime*.

[30] Letters to Dobell, January 18, 1875, quoted by Salt, *op. cit.*, p. 125; May 18, 1875, quoted *loc. cit.*; July 9, 1875, quoted *op. cit.*, p. 126; August 24, 1875, quoted *loc. cit.* Thomson's diary for 1875, which might give more information, has been "lost." One suspects that it was destroyed by his friends, who saw no reason to preserve more records of this unfortunate incident than were already available to the public.

generosity over a long period of time, Thomson was hardly in a position to make an issue of a small debt, however legitimate. Yet he needed the money urgently, so urgently that he went so far as to threaten legal action.

The account of the quarrel might well end at this point were it not for the sentimental and widely circulated sequel that, when Thomson saw Bradlaugh being forcibly ejected from the Parliament Buildings in 1881, he made an impulsive move to go to the assistance of his former friend, thus proving his continued loyalty.[31] This story must be taken with skepticism, for sprinkled throughout the diaries of the years following the quarrel and even in his printed articles are savagely caustic remarks. Typical is the somewhat angry diary entry referring to an arrest and imprisonment of Bradlaugh: "The imbecile bigots have been playing his game, . . . given him twenty-fold notoriety, his very breath of life." [32] That concerned with the incident at Parliament notes almost gleefully, "Brad's attempt on House of Commons. Grand field day for JWB, Percy, and I." [33] On the other hand a few comments give evidence that at times his bitter animosity was

---

[31] John M. Robertson, quoted by Hypatia Bradlaugh Bonner, *Charles Bradlaugh,* II, 287, told the story thus: "I have been told that James Thomson, the poet, the estranged friend of Bradlaugh's youth, was among those at the gates; that he turned pale at the sight of the struggling group; and that his companions could hardly withhold him by force from rushing to his old comrade's help." Salt, in the 1914 edition of the *Life,* took the story from Robertson almost verbatim, adding a quotation from J. H. MacCarthy's *England under Gladstone:* "Thomson had been of old a friend and follower of Mr. Bradlaugh; their ways of thought had varied of late, and their paths had separated; but here, in the moment of difficulty, Thomson came to do all he could for the cause he believed to be just—the cause of his old friend."

[32] Diary, June 24, 1880.

[33] Diary, August 3, 1881.

softened, not, I would say, by loyalty, but by a sudden mood of regretful disillusionment. A vitriolic attack on Bradlaugh in a letter to *The Secularist* he ended on such a note: "Such cowardice and meanness are so unworthy of the Mr. Bradlaugh I once knew. . . . All his old courage seems to have evaporated." [34]

Thomson's second quarrel was with G. W. Foote in 1879. The wrangle caused by Foote's failure to pay Thomson for copy received ran on for two full years, during which neither man acted well. The affair makes Thomson appear mercenary in the extreme; one wishes he had been able to cross the item off his books as a bad debt and forget it. But this he could not do, for by that time his need for money was greater than it had ever been. During the period of protracted bickering *Cope's* was discontinued and Thomson was left without any sure market for his work, without any generous editor to whom to appeal for an advance. In justice to Foote, it should be added that, however badly he may have behaved during the quarrel, he did not allow the affair to pervert the memoir he wrote of Thomson after his death. Unlike Hypatia Bradlaugh Bonner, who as a child had often been made happy by Thomson, Foote did not become vindictive or unfair.

It has been suggested that these two quarrels were caused by the psychopathic suspiciousness common to dipsomaniacs. Perhaps there is truth in the theory, but one can hardly accept it without reservation since there is no evidence whatsoever that Thomson quarreled with anyone else. His close intimacy with the Holyoake and Wright families continued uninterrupted by so much as a disagreement; his business relations

---

[34] *The Secularist*, April 22, 1876.

with John Fraser of *Cope's* remained excellent; he worked and consulted with Dobell in complete harmony; and finally he formed a new friendship with the Barrs which lasted until his death. If it is true that he became psychopathically suspicious, it certainly cannot be assumed that he became generally unpleasant and truculent.

Thomson's lodgings during the last seven of these eight years were in a way a symbol of his defeated hopes, his abasing poverty, his wretched health.[35] Both sides of the narrow street were lined solidly with six-story red brick buildings, and across the end near which he lived was another row of red brick buildings. A block or two in the other direction was the University College Hospital, from which came the depressing odor of antiseptics. In the winter the sky hung low over the street as though to close in on it, and in the summer the heat lay still and heavy on it. From his window Thomson, who loved the country, could see no green thing and could catch only narrow glimpses of the sky.

The location had advantages, however. Not only was it a five minutes' walk from the British Museum, but it was close to the home of Theodore Wright, who had married Austin Holyoake's widow. There Thomson spent so many of his evenings that he was almost a member of the family, even as he had been at the Bradlaugh home some twelve or fifteen years earlier. In both instances his frustrated desire to be a part of a family was pathetically apparent.

Included in the diaries of these years, along with their sadder story, is the account of Thomson's happier days. During the winter he managed at least twice a month to attend some

---

[35] 35 Alfred Street, Gower Street, later renamed and renumbered 7 Huntley Street.

musical entertainment. This pleasure was his only extravagance during these years except his tobacco, and a small one it was, since seats for the opera were only one and six and for the Monday "pop" concerts at St. James's Hall but a shilling. In the spring he escaped occasionally from his red brick walls to Kew Gardens, where he enjoyed the broad green lawns, the avenues of tall limes and chestnuts, and the spring flowers. Or if he could not go to Kew, he walked along the river to watch the trees breaking into bud, the pigeons strutting about, and the return of activity on the Thames as the freshly painted river barges began to hoist their big brown sails.

It was during these years that Thomson came to enjoy for the first time a certain amount of social contact with literary figures. Earlier, to be sure, he had had some fleeting connections. Late in 1869 he had been a breakfast guest of James Anthony Froude, but the meeting had been of the semi-business author-editor sort and was not repeated.[36] And in April, 1873, he had accepted an invitation to call on William M. Rossetti; [37] the contact, however, was not continued [38]

[36] Diary, November 19, 1869, quoted by Salt, *op. cit.,* p. 58.

[37] In the account of Thomson that Rossetti wrote for Salt, quoted *op. cit.,* pp. 70 ff., he commented that he thought the date "must have been" before April, 1872. Thomson's letter of acceptance of the invitation, however, is dated April 22, 1873.

[38] Rossetti's accounts of his contacts with Thomson lead, by implication, to some confusion. In *Some Reminiscences* (1906), II, 500, he wrote, "During my married life my wife as well as myself was wishful to cultivate his acquaintance, and he was in our house some half-dozen times, meeting friends at dinner once or twice." Such a comment would seem to imply that Rossetti sought Thomson's friendship. The earlier account written for Salt, undated but referred to in *Some Reminiscences,* implies rather the opposite. The tone of the whole is patronizing and the sketch deals at length with Thomson's manners and his pronunciation of *h.* It ends with this paragraph: "The whole of my personal acquaintance with Thomson may have amounted to some half-dozen

despite the fact that the two men corresponded from early 1872 into 1881, to a large extent on the subject of Rossetti's work on Shelley.[39] Late in December, 1876, however, Thomson met Miss Mathilde Blinde. Through her he became acquainted with the Madox Browns, the Ford Heuffers, Arthur William Edgar O'Shaughnessy, and Philip Bourke Marston and saw more of the Rossettis. From New Year's Day, 1877, he was a fairly frequent guest at the parties especially of Miss Blinde and the Madox Browns; [40] but it is indicative of his somewhat peripheral position in the group that except for the parties he apparently had contact with only one member, Philip Bourke Marston, whom he occasionally saw and talked with alone.[41]

Meeting these people at first pleased and stimulated Thomson, as is evidenced by his unusually long and enthusiastic

---

interviews. I don't remember what may have been the last date when I met him; probably not later than 1876 or 1877. He and I were always on the best of terms; and we had occasion to correspond every now and then up to I dare say a couple of years preceding his death." Checking Thomson's diaries, one concludes that the latter account more closely expressed Rossetti's attitude and is the more accurate. Thomson did meet Rossetti some half-dozen times, but, except for the 1873 meeting, only after contact had been made through Miss Blinde, in December, 1876, or January, 1877.

[39] Of this correspondence all that now remain are the letters quoted by Salt and those included in the privately printed *Shelley, a Poem; with Other Writings Relating to Shelley*. These are as follows: in Salt, letters dated February 8, March 2, April 10, August 5, 1872; April 2, April 22, November 12 (includes reference to notes on Shelley sent to Rossetti in July), 1873; January 30, 1874; December 21, 1875; March 6, April 7, December 15, 1880; July 7, 1881. In the *Shelley* are six of those used by Salt (February 8, March 2, April 10, August 5, 1872, and April 2 and November 11, 1873) plus two more from Thomson to Rossetti, April 21, 1872, and April 18, 1873, both concerning notes on Shelley, and two from Rossetti to Thomson, April 28, 1872, and April 21, 1873.

[40] Diaries of 1877 through 1881.

[41] Diary, August 20 and October 15, 1880.

diary entry concerning an early party.[42] His report of his meeting with Froude and his earliest letters to Rossetti show that they were the sort whom he had always been eager to know and with whom he would have had more in common than with the Secularist journalists and reformers who had been almost his only friends for twenty years. But the later dull, purely factual accounts of the parties indicate that the stimulation was soon gone. The new contacts had come too late. Thomson was worn out physically and too disheartened to respond. The creative energies that such people might have helped fire were all but dead. Although he continued to accept the invitations of the group for the next four years, he seems to have preferred a quiet afternoon of relaxing tea-table chat with the Wrights to an evening of exciting intellectual discussion with the Madox Brown group, and it is clear that he felt no regret when he was too ill to attend the parties.[43] If, in 1873, Rossetti had offered him the social opportunity which Miss Blinde gave him, the experience of being with literary figures might have meant much to him, might have alleviated the loneliness he always felt. By this time it meant little.

It was also during this period that Thomson began corresponding with George Meredith.[44] How extensive the exchange of letters may have been is not known; but if the three remaining are fair samples, it can be asserted that the novelist was generous with both praise and encouragement.[45] In June,

[42] Diary, January 4, 1877.

[43] Diary, June 7, 1878.

[44] Salt, *op. cit.*, p. 137.

[45] Meredith, *Letters,* I, 302, 303, and 307–308. These letters are all quoted in full or in part by Salt, *op. cit.*, pp. 137, 152–153, and 153–154

1880, Thomson spent a day with Meredith at Box Hill, "A day to be marked with a white stone," he wrote in his diary; [46] and again the following year he was a guest at Box Hill.[47] But the correspondence and the visits did not bespeak a real friendship however much they were a source of pride and pleasure to Thomson.

The year 1880 brought Thomson a new experience and for a brief period new hope and strength. After five years of difficulties and disappointments in the search for a publisher, he wrote in his diary on March 4 the modest entry: "Dobell having arranged with Mr. Reeves for publication of a small tentative volume (six full sheets = 192 pages; exclusive of Title pages, Dedication, and Contents), Reeves put it at once to press with Messrs. Ballantyne, Hanson and Co., Edinboro'. On Thursday, 4th March 1880, I got first proof of 16 pp. Volume to be entitled 'The City of Dreadful Night, and other Poems.' " [48] There were to be five hundred copies at five shillings, and forty on large paper at ten.[49] He continued: "I take no share of risk and have one-third of profit (if any). Fair for a first book, as I have certain gain of an independent name." Thus the first mention of Thomson's, or rather Dobell's, success in finding a publisher was made only after plans had materialized and the first proof sheets had

---

respectively. Other letters of Meredith concerning Thomson, written to Salt, are to be found in the *Letters*, II, 413, 413–414, and 437.

[46] Diary, June 29, 1880.

[47] Diary, September 13, 1881.

[48] Mr. Reeves put up the capital for the venture despite the fact that there was apparently little chance of a reasonable return. For such generosity and faith he justly called forth the praise both of Bertram Dobell and in later years of Percy Dobell.

[49] Actually 1000 of the five-shilling copies were printed.

arrived. Apparently Thomson had become so disillusioned with publishers that he was unwilling to note his hopes even in his diaries until he had tangible evidence that they would work out. The diaries for the next week or two are all concerned with reading proof, gathering translations of Heine from *The Secularist* to be included in the volume, examining sample book bindings, and having pictures taken.[50]

When the book was issued, the reviewers damned "The City" almost universally, reserving what little commendation they had for the other poems in the volume.[51] But Thomson was neither surprised nor disheartened by such a reception; he had more or less expected it. Of more significance to him than critics' reviews was a letter from Meredith:

> I have not found the line I would propose to recast. I have found many pages which no other English poet could have written. Nowhere is the verse feeble, nowhere is the expression insufficient; the majesty of the line has always its full colouring, and marches under a banner. And you accomplish this effect with the utmost sobriety, with absolute self-mastery. . . . There is a massive impressiveness in [section xxi of "The City"] that goes beyond Dürer, and takes it into the upper regions where

---

[50] As a matter of fact no picture of Thomson appeared in any of the volumes published during his lifetime.

[51] George Saintsbury in the *Academy*, June 12, 1880, was the most encouraging: he recognized the merits of "The City" and pointed out only genuine faults. Joel Benton in *Appleton's Journal*, May, 1881, called Thomson insincere, assuming that he was "well and healthy," able to consume good meals, and no worse off than his fellows. The reviewer in the *Athenaeum*, May 1, 1881, felt that Thomson was merely following the fashion of pessimistic poetry and complained "To conscientiously read ['The City'] through is a weary task." The *London Quarterly Review* critic frankly admitted what the others implied: "We start from the basis that pessimism is heresy."

poetry is the sublimation of the mind of man, the voice of our highest.[52]

In spite of the reviews the project turned out to be financially successful; in August Thomson received ten pounds on account from Reeves, *"unasked."* [53] But the success was not great enough to relieve his poverty to any extent, for it was in this same year and after the publication that he was forced twice to ask Fraser for advances.[54] Nevertheless Thomson was extremely gratified and wrote in his diary, "N.B. Other publishers all firm that *no* vol. of verses, however good, can now pay its expenses, unless bearing one of three or four famous or popular names. Yet this vol. by an unknown writer and burdened with the heavy dead weight of the somber and atheistical and generally incomprehensible CDN *has* paid its expenses." [55] Moreover the sale continued good for several months, especially in Cambridge and Oxford, a fact which so pleased Thomson that he noted it in his diary.[56]

Within a few weeks Dobell and Reeves asked for material for a second volume.[57] Thomson immediately started collecting and arranging poems for it, and in October, 1880, *Vane's Story, Weddah and Om-el-Bonain, and Other Poems* appeared.[58] Although the book did not sell as well as its predecessor, Thomson set to work preparing a third volume, a

---

[52] Dated April 27, 1880, quoted by Salt, *op. cit.*, p. 153.

[53] Diary, August 17, 1880.

[54] Diary, June 28 and October 10, 1880.

[55] Diary, August 17, 1880.

[56] Diary, January 7, 1881.

[57] Diary, June 13, 1880.

[58] October, 1880, is the date assigned by Salt and supported by references to the publication in Thomson's letters. The date on the title page, however, is 1881.

collection of prose. It was issued in April, 1881, under the title *Essays and Phantasies.* Its poor reception was partially justified, for inferior essays counterbalanced some of Thomson's finest prose, and even the best did not appeal to the taste of the reading public.[59]

Thomson's new strength, born of the excitement of preparing and having a volume of verse published, was short-lived. He was hopeful and even enthusiastic while he was working on *The City of Dreadful Night and Other Poems,* but as soon as it appeared, the nervous energy which had kept him going ran out. He seemed to derive very little pleasure from the appearance of the two following books; the few remarks concerning them in the diaries are as unenthusiastic as the daily record of the weather. The good fortune of publication came too late to be of permanent value. Only forty-seven, Thomson was already in such poor physical condition that nothing more than a brief revival of his strength was possible.

---

[59] These were the only three volumes published during Thomson's life. The first was sold out, but the others were not, and in 1890 the warehouse in which the remainders of the 1000-copy editions of *Vane's Story* and *Essays and Phantasies* were stored was burned and approximately half of each edition was destroyed. In the same warehouse were also posthumous volumes: *A Voice from the Nile and Other Poems,* 1884, 1000-copy edition, about one-half destroyed; *Satires and Profanities,* 1884, 3000-copy edition, nearly all destroyed; *The City of Dreadful Night and Other Poems,* 2nd ed., 1000 copies, part destroyed. About 600 of the 1000 copies of Salt's 1889 edition of the *Life of James Thomson (B.V.)* were also destroyed. Later publications include *The Poetical Works of James Thomson, The City of Dreadful Night and Other Poems,* a two-volume work published in 1895; *Biographical and Critical Studies,* 1896; *Poems, Essays, and Fragments,* 1892; and the Leopardi translations, 1905. The first American edition of *The City of Dreadful Night* was published in 1892. These constitute the major editions of Thomson's works.

Thomson's work for the *National Reformer* and for *The Secularist* [60] was of the sort he had done since his arrival in London in 1862: book reviews, reports of Secularist lectures, discussions of political affairs of special interest to Secularist readers, and occasional essays prompted by personal interests. For *Cope's Tobacco Plant*, however, his work was of a different character, for that journal released him from certain policy obligations that he had known under the Secularist papers and at the same time imposed others on him. To understand these, indeed to understand some of the work Thomson did for *Cope's*, one needs some acquaintance with the publication.

*Cope's Tobacco Plant* was a monthly periodical put out by the Liverpool firm, Cope's Tobacco Plant, primarily for carrying advertisements; but in addition it also printed long serialized articles on such subjects as the history or the culture of tobacco. Such articles naturally occupied the greater number of inches in the journal; but, as Thomson remarked, *Cope's* was "one of the more daring and original publications of the day" and carried almost as much copy on literature as on tobacco. It regularly ran a column, called "Mixtures," on literary subjects, and a book review section, "The Smoke-Room Table"; it printed long articles on literary figures; and each year it offered its subscribers a "Christmas Card," an elaborate pamphlet done in the style of a famous literary work.

For the trade section Thomson did three major articles, "Tobacco Smuggling in the Last Generation," "The Tobacco

---

[60] A diary entry of March 21, 1880, shows Thomson's attitude toward both: "Hitherto anonymous, and in such papers as the N.R. and Sec.; reference to which would have been anything but a recommendation."

Duties," and "Tobacco Legislation in the Three Kingdoms." [61]
And at least two of the "Christmas Cards" were his: *The Pilgrimage to Saint Nicotine,* after the *Canterbury Tales,* and *The Pursuit of Diva Nicotine,* after Sir Noel Paton's *Pursuit of Pleasure.*[62] But the greater part of his work was for the literary sections of the journal. He occasionally substituted for the regular writer of the "Mixtures" and also did routine

---

[61] "Smuggling" ran to seven installments, "Duties" to three, and "Legislation" to thirteen.

[62] I have been unable to find a copy of *The Pursuit,* but there is one of *The Pilgrimage* at the Huntington Library in San Marino, California. The catalogue card "attributes" *The Pilgrimage* to Thomson; his letters and diaries offer conclusive proof it was really his work.

*The Pilgrimage* is a twenty-nine-page pamphlet, issued for subscribers at twopence. The cover shows a sketch of St. Nicotine opening a door with a key. Inside is a larger illustration in black and white, signed G. Pipeshank, done in part after Blake's *Canterbury Pilgrims,* showing sixty-five numbered pilgrims. The prose prologue explains that whereas Rabelais took his followers to the Shrine of La Dive Bouteille, Thomson will take his to that of St. Nicotine. Then there comes "The Pilgrimage to Saint Nicotine of the Holy Herb," all in verse, divided into two parts: "The Pilgrims" and "The Saint and His Shrine." The first part is that printed in Volume I of *The Poetical Works* under the title of "The Prologue to the Pilgrimage to Saint Nicotine of the Holy Herb." Part I, the Pilgrims, is followed by a key to the thirty characters used by Thomson: the Knight is Carlyle; the Squire, Ruskin; the Yeoman, Froude; the Reve, Charles Reade; the Poet, Tennyson; the Clerke, Newman; the Carpenter, Holman Hunt; the Dyere, Gustave Dore, etc. Part II, "The Saint and His Shrine," tells the legend of the martyrdom of St. Nicotine and the devotion of his apostles.

The verse is all iambic pentameter couplets, with slightly archaic diction, but there is no real attempt to imitate Chaucerian language, style, or grammar. The lightness of tone and the sly bits of satire are, however, Chaucerian in spirit. There is evidence that, although Thomson did not try to follow Chaucer closely, he spent much time in preparing to do this piece of work: he cited Tyrwhitt's rejection of one distich and disagreed with an interpretation of Stottard; he believed Blake correct in omitting the comma between the two words *webbe* and *deyer* and agreed that there should be but twenty-nine characters exclusive of the poet.

book reviews, especially those of the English Men of Letters series, for the "Smoke-Room Table." His biggest task, however, was writing the articles on various authors. The greater part of every one of these essays is biographical, yet their chief value for a student of Thomson lies in the few sentences or paragraphs of criticism he introduced in each. It is, therefore, convenient to classify them as criticism and consider them with his more purely critical works.

Thomson's earlier criticism has been left until this chapter because only by viewing the whole of his scattered and varied excursions into the field can one see the pattern in it. Moreover the early criticism, though no less important than that of this period, is much smaller in quantity.

Thomson's first attempt, "Notes on Emerson," 1858, was a short analysis of two or three of Emerson's characteristics. This was followed in 1859 by "A Few Words about Burns," an essay of a similar sort, only slightly more ambitious. Then in 1860 came "Shelley," the most important because, in addition to its careful and sympathetic analysis of Shelley's poetry, it includes the most explicit statement of Thomson's standards of literary evaluation, his four tests of great poetry. The first of these tests is that subjects must be great intellectually and morally; proper subjects include the existence of God, the moral law of the universe, the independent being of what is called the material world, and the perfectibility of man. Second, the subjects must be treated with corresponding intellectual greatness, that is, with sincerity and magnanimity of conception. Third, they must be handled with pure, noble, and "generous moral emotions," which include love of one's fellows, self-sacrificing sympathy, pity, hatred of cruelty and fraud, and reverence of truth and goodness. Fourth, and most important in his statement, great poetry must be inspired, must be "always from within, not from without." Further definition of inspiration Thomson failed to give concisely, but he made his concept clear in several pages of discussion and by quoting from Shelley's translation of the "Ion": "The authors of those great poems which we admire . . . utter their beautiful melodies of verse in a state of inspiration, and, as it were, *possessed* by a spirit not their own . . . nor can [a poet] compose anything worth calling poetry until he becomes inspired and, as it were, mad. . . ."

"The Poems of William Blake," 1864, Thomson's next piece of criticism, is more important in the story of his philosophic development than it is in an account of his standards of judgment for much of it is heavily underlined with pantheism, a concept he was soon to abandon.[63] The first part is a thoughtful analysis of Blake's poetry. This is followed by Thomson's attempt to establish the standard of "simplicity":

> The essence of [Blake's] poetry is mysticism, and the essence of this mysticism is simplicity. . . . It sees, and is continually rapturous with seeing, everywhere correspondence, kindred, identity, not only in the things and creatures of earth, but in all things and creatures and beings of hell and earth and heaven, up to one father (or interiorly to one soul) of all.

In the last part of the essay Thomson applied this test of "simplicity" to ten English and American poets. But the significant point is that in the application he several times used

---

[63] Salt dated "Blake" as 1865; in "A Strange Book," however, Thomson gave the date as 1864.

the first of the four tests outlined in "Shelley," that proper subjects are great intellectually and morally, in place of or in conjunction with the test of "simplicity." This is especially true in his disparaging remarks, as in his comment that Scott's poetry was "of action, not of thought." Fundamentally his first consideration was whether a poem had adequate thought content, was intellectual; the concept of "simplicity" is but a pantheistic, and temporary, veneer laid on that standard. It was expressed but once more, in the section on Poets in "Open Secret Societies," 1865.

Thomson's last critical essay of these early years was "An Evening with Spenser," 1865, noteworthy for its short but imaginative and sympathetic characterization of the Elizabethans. From that date until 1874, he did no more criticism except routine book reviews for the *National Reformer*, few of which were more than slight summaries and none of which was of lasting value. In 1874, however, he began the biographical studies with "Walt Whitman," which appeared in the *National Reformer*. By no means the best of the group, it nevertheless set the pattern. Because, as Dobell commented, its avowed purpose was to give English readers "as vivid an idea as possible of Whitman's personality and writings," it relied heavily on quotations from Whitman and Whitman biographers.[64] In the last few pages, however, there is some criticism introduced by way of characterizing the poetry. Such is the comment following a quotation from "Reconciliation": "All these and many other wonderful chants, wonderful for poetry, grandeur, courage, sincerity, veracity, all-embracing sympathy, seem less works of art than immediate outgrowths

---

[64] Dobell, "Introduction," *Walt Whitman: The Man and the Poet*, p. xxxv.

of nature. . . ." Such is the type of almost incidental criticism that marks the biographical studies.

"Whitman" was followed in 1876 by "Heine," which, despite its excellence as a biographical sketch, is almost completely without criticism, and then in the years 1876 through 1880 by the studies done for *Cope's:* "Saint Amant," "Rabelais," "Ben Jonson," "John Wilson and the 'Noctes Ambrosianae,' " "James Hogg, the Ettrick Shepherd," and a second "Walt Whitman." [65]

Of these the best are the "Rabelais" and the "Jonson," both of which are marked by such vitality that one recognizes the immense pleasure Thomson took in the research and writing. The first half of the long Jonson essay (160 pages), based on William Gifford, Francis Cunningham, Drummond of Hawthornden, and the entire body of Jonson's works, far from being a simple summary of secondary sources, shows careful use of evidence and weighing of authority; the second half, wherein Thomson allowed his humor free play, is an exhaustive study of all references to tobacco in Jonson's works. The essay includes, however, only a few sentences of criticism, too few considering their quality. Such a one as that on Jonson's prose deserves amplification: "We can recognize that it is truly admirable—terse, unaffected, perspicuous, sincere, weighty with knowledge and thought; and so little out of date that it might have been written yesterday."

---

[65] This second, more than half again as long as the first, condenses much of the biographical material offered in the first but adds many details about Whitman's work in the hospitals during the Civil War and quotes extensively from his *Memoranda during the War*, which, one judges, Thomson had not seen at the time he wrote the first essay. These two essays were published together under the title *Walt Whitman: The Man and the Poet* by Dobell in 1910.

The "Rabelais," on the other hand, contains several pages of criticism per se, more than any other of these biographical studies. This is marked, as are most of his critical essays, by comparisons. One from the "Rabelais" shows especially well the sort of analysis he was capable of but too infrequently and too sparingly employed:

> Both see with a vision that cannot be muffled through all the hypocrisies and falsehoods, all the faults and follies of mankind; but the scorn of Rabelais rolls out in jolly laughter, while the scorn of Swift is a *saeva indignatio*—the one is vented in wine, the other in vitriol. Both are prodigal in dirt, having an immense and varied assortment always on hand, to be supplied at the shortest notice. But the dirt of Swift, in spite of all that has been said against it, is in most cases distinctly moral, being heaped on immorality and vileness in order to render them the more repulsive. . . . The dirt of Rabelais, on the other hand, when he does not intentionally besmear himself with it in order to appear a buffoon when most audaciously sarcastic and heterodox, had nothing to do with morality or immorality, but is simply the dirt of a child. . . .

Shortly after starting on the biographical studies, Thomson began to write a few essays of a more critical nature, comparable in their analytic quality to his first two pieces, the "Emerson" and the "Burns." Three of these were primarily reviews of novels of Meredith, but the first especially contains some genuine criticism. This, "Beauchamp's Career," 1876, consists, so far as number of words goes, mostly of quotations; but the quotations were chosen to substantiate and illustrate Thomson's analysis of Meredith's outstanding characteristics: his "depth and scope and subtlety of intellect," his appeal "to the conscience residing in thoughtfulness," his "heavy and frequent demands on active imagination," his ability "to suggest by flying touches." This method of generalization backed by example is typical of Thomson's criticism at its best; but often, and in this case, he erred seriously by stating his judgments so briefly that they fail to attract the consideration due them. This fault is even more evident in the two other essays on Meredith, "An Old New Book (*The Ordeal of Richard Feverel*)," 1879, and "George Meredith's New Work (*The Egoist*)," 1880, both of which are inferior to the earlier essay.[66]

A second group of three essays was focused on Browning.[67] The first of these, "Pacciarotto, by Robert Browning," 1876, is a good piece of analysis but comparatively slight because limited to those "personal characteristics . . . [which] have not . . . been so plainly discovered in any of the author's previous works." A later essay, " 'The Ring and the Book,' " 1881, though overloaded with quotations, is better by virtue of its last pages, which include Thomson's reasons for his admiration of both Meredith and Browning:

> I know of but one other living English poet to whom we can turn for the like supreme analytic synthesis, the patient analysis of a most subtle and unappeasable intellect, the organic synthesis of a most vivid and dramatic imagination; which the better critics at length

---

[66] Thomson also did a page-long review of *Beauchamp's Career* for *Cope's*. All four of these pieces on Meredith were collected and privately printed as a limited edition of fifty copies in London in 1909, under the title *James Thomson ("B.V.") on George Meredith*.

[67] Chronologically the two later of these essays belong to the following chapter but for convenience they are included here.

publicly recognized in the "Egoist," after almost ignoring or wholly underrating them in the "Modern Love" . . . and other great original works of George Meredith.

But best is the last, the "Notes on the Genius of Robert Browning," 1882.[68] Perhaps because it was written to be read at the Browning Society and Thomson could therefore assume an audience more acquainted with his subject than the readers of periodicals, he expanded his ideas more fully and used less quotation, thus achieving a better balance and doing more justice to himself. In spite of the brevity of the essay, he capably handled seven "notes." Typical is that on "Browning's manliness," which he summarized thus:

> With a masculine soul for passion, a masculine intellect for thought, and a masculine genius for imagination, all on a vast scale, and all fused together in one intense fire when the theme is great and imperious, we have the highest results of which poetry is capable; and such results I recognize in the noblest poems and passages of Browning. . . .

In this whole period there is but one essay which, like the "Shelley" and "Blake," deals with the theory of poetry or standards of judgment, namely, "A Strange Book," 1879. The latter and shorter part of this long essay on James John Garth Wilkinson's poems, *Improvisations from the Spirit,* is concerned with the poems themselves; the first and more significant part treats with sympathy but also with some adverse comment

---

[68] Prepared at the request of F. J. Furnival for the Browning Society and read, presumably by someone else, at the meeting of that group January 27, 1882.

Wilkinson's theory of poetry, that, having chosen and written down a theme, one becomes an instrument of the "Spirit" and merely writes those "impressions" it dictates. This idea of inspiration, stripped of its verbal trappings, is the same that Thomson had used in "Shelley"; indeed, in discussing it he used some of the same quotations from Plato he had used in that earlier essay.[69] Moreover it is clear that his basic concept of inspiration had not changed fundamentally, but there are three points which distinguish the later expression of it. Least important, perhaps, is that in "A Strange Book" the older and more experienced Thomson insisted on much careful revision and correction following initial quick writing, a subject ignored in the early essay. And, as should be expected, all pantheistic coloring is gone; there is no suggestion of a universal soul. But most important is an idea tucked away in a footnote:

> To myself, ecstasy, trance, inspiration, vision, revelation, are no less simply human and natural, though so much less common, than sleep and waking; are just as susceptible of scientific explanation, though our science is not yet subtle and comprehensive enough to pervade them, as spring-tides or summer flowering and fruitage or the *aurora borealis*.

This is the mature Thomson, the Thomson of "The City of Dreadful Night."

Because I have endeavored to hold quotations to a reasonable number, the above consideration perhaps fails to show

---

[69] In "Shelley" Thomson had used Shelley's translation of the *Ion;* in "A Strange Book" he used the Jowett translation.

clearly the relation of the standards he actually used to those
he explicitly stated in 1860 in the "Shelley." By substituting
for a list of quotations a list of his words of commendation it
is possible, however, to achieve this end. Of the four standards
affirmed in the "Shelley," the last, that poetry must be inspired, Thomson used unmistakably only in the three essays
in which he dealt with inspiration per se: "Shelley," "Blake,"
and "A Strange Book." Elsewhere he occasionally seems to
imply that a work was or was not inspired, but the application
of inspiration as a test is not explicit. The other three standards, however, he used consistently and clearly, expanding
their application to include prose as well as poetry. His demand
that proper subjects be great intellectually and morally is reflected in the group of words which appear and reappear as
the highest praise in his criticism from the "Emerson" of 1859
to the "Browning" of 1882: intellectual, thought, vision, analysis, keen insight, and world knowledge. A second set re-
flects, though out of context less clearly than those just cited,
his demand for intellectual greatness of treatment: manliness, vitality, robustness, intense life, vigor, directness, open-
air relish, pithy, vulgar, manly relish, lusty, savage, virility,
power, masculinity, bigness, full-blooded, swiftness, energy,
strength, and fire. And the third group stems from his requi-
site generous moral emotions: imagination, sympathy, humanity, and democracy. The application is seen in the following
typical quotations:

> Without going back to Shakespeare and Bacon, we may
> select works from a literary epoch upon which we affect
> to look down, works such as Pope's *Essay on Man* or
> Swift's *Tale of a Tub,* wherein nearly every sentence had

required a distinct intellectual effort, and which thus, whatever their faults, shame by their powerful virility our effeminate modern books.[70]

Scarcely any other artist in verse of the same rank has ever lived on such scanty revenues of thought (both pure, and applied or mixed) as Tennyson. . . . He is a pensioner on the thought of his age. . . . Nothing gives one a keener insight into the want of robustness in the educated English intellect of the age than the fact that nine-tenths of our best known literary men look upon him as a profound philosopher.[71]

Similar applications may be noted in earlier quotations. Thus without mechanically applying the standards as he did to Shelley's work, he continued to use them.[72]

The significance of the fact that Thomson had such standards as his bases of literary judgment and used them for more than twenty years is obvious, but it may be further pointed by noting his omissions. He did not, for example, mention plot or character as such when writing of Meredith's novels; he did not consider character or dramatic qualities in Browning's poetry. Only very seldom, and then in a cursory and general fashion, did he comment on a writer's skill or craftsmanship; never did he stop to analyze that skill. Thomson's first thought was to examine the intellectual content of a work and the intellectual qualities of its treatment; that is, the basic concept, to meet his approval, had to be intellectual and the

---

[70] "Per Contra."

[71] "Blake."

[72] Expressions of disparagement include the following: entanglement of feminine draperies, soft, exquisite, weak, young ladyish affectation, sentimental, nervous, hysterics.

treatment had to be logical and intellectually honest. And his second consideration was the imaginative sympathy displayed. "The City of Dreadful Night" of course meets both tests, and so does Thomson himself. Here in his criticism are seen not merely his ideals of literature but his ideals of human conduct. Thomson's story is that of a man who believed in reason rather than emotion, whose intellectual honesty never flagged, and whose sympathy for his fellows warmed both his life and his work. When one reads the criticism, one's understanding of the man grows.

In this period fall two of Thomson's four phantasies, "The Fair of St. Sylvester," 1875, and "In Our Forest of the Past," 1877.[73] "The Fair" is a puzzling work, for, despite several excellent descriptive passages of an imaginative nature, it is laden with cryptic remarks and some of the symbolism is so obscure as to be meaningless. Salt characterized it "a sort of prose reproduction of *Vane's Story*," but with this I cannot agree, for it lacks the intensity of feeling, the philosophic implications, and the personal experience that went into the better parts of the poem. These elements are, however, found in "In Our Forest," one of Thomson's finest achievements in prose. In this allegory, suggested by the *Divine Comedy*, Thomson is led through the forest of the dead, where he sees those who had been deprived by nature of the chance to live a full life, the halt and the blind; those who had been deprived by men, the oppressed and the imprisoned; those who had been deprived by themselves, the monks and the dreamers. All moan their "frustrate lives." Then he is led to another

---

[73] The first, "A Lady of Sorrow," 1862–1864, has been considered in Chapter II. The second, "A Walk Abroad," 1866, is a trivial and unimportant work.

part of the forest, where he sees those who had the opportunity and the wisdom and the will to live fully. These smile quietly in their sleep.

Despite the closing ideas in the work, unique in Thomson's writings, that man rather than nature may be responsible for at least some of his ills and that there may be a possibility of self-improvement, the whole is presented in a spirit of apathy more sustained and more consistent than is found in any of his earlier writings.[74] Although he had insisted on the wisdom of an apathetic attitude towards life, he had never been able to attain and hold it for any length of time. An undertone of rebellion, though impotent and conscious of its impotence, was almost always present, usually faint but occasionally strident, as in the dialogue and the second cathedral scene in "The City." In "In Our Forest" there is no such note; there is only quiet, unstruggling despair.

This despair is intensified by the rhythmic quality of the poetic prose in which the work is written. The rhythm, long and smooth, flows with the evenness of definitely phrased music, yet it avoids mellifluence and monotony. It is achieved by skillfully manipulated parallelism—parallelism of phrase,

---

[74] Of this curious passage of only just over a hundred words, Salt wrote: "The close of *In Our Forest of the Past* is remarkable as containing almost the only passage in Thomson's writings where a belief in the possibility of human progress is distinctly hinted at, and where, in direct contradiction to the general drift of his doctrine, Man, and not Nature, is declared to be responsible for the burden of human suffering." But another writer, identified only as "B.E.," who prepared the introduction of *The Story of a Famous Old Jewish Firm and Other Pieces in Prose and Rime* when it was reprinted as the Leek Bijou Reprints No. VI in 1883, made these amazing statements: "[Thomson's] confidence in the beneficence of NATURE never falters; he is ever sensible of HER wisdom, outraged by the ignorance of MAN. . . . Intense is his love of NATURE; perfect his trust in her."

of clause, of sentence—and by repetition of words and phrases. It is carried so far that it gives the effect of stanzas, each similarly introduced, each of approximately equal length, and each ending with the refrain, only slightly varied, "They moan their frustrate lives." The ornamentation consists almost entirely of this marked rhythm; the few figures are short and not particularly striking, and the diction is never "poetic" or ostentatiously unusual. The content and beauty of treatment are such as would make this phantasy noteworthy at any time; coming as it does in these years when Thomson was writing almost nothing of an imaginative nature it is especially important.

One more piece of prose remains to be considered in this period, "La Tentation de Saint Antoine par Gustave Flaubert," 1876, written only two years after the book had first appeared in France and before any English translation had been published. A strange mixture of criticism, summary, and translation, it might properly have been discussed with Thomson's other critical works were it not for the fact that its particular value lies in the translation. After a short discussion of *Madame Bovary,* a few remarks on *Salammbô* and *L'Education sentimentale,* and an explanation of Flaubert's method of handling the theme of *La Tentation,* Thomson proceeded with the major part of the essay, which might be described as a condensed translation. This he wrote in a style very close to that of Flaubert, skillfully translating the colorful descriptions in unusual, exotic language, comparable in flavor with that of the original. In commenting on Flaubert's style, Thomson spoke of its "semi-barbaric music, sonorous and vibrant, as the measured clashing of cymbals, the persistent slow beating of gongs, the chattering tumult of trumpets swaying

[ 153 ]

immense armies on the march." And this music he captured and for the moment made his own with rare felicity. Thus to preserve the quality of the original in a condensation is a task Thomson imposed on himself in no other of his translations and his success attests further to his ability in the field. It is unfortunate that the piece has never been reprinted, was not, indeed, even mentioned by Salt, for it is worthy of attention.

In contrast to the great bulk of prose was the small amount of poetry. This discrepancy worried and depressed Thomson. Following the appearance of "The City" he published almost no poetry except reprints of earlier work which had appeared for the most part in the *National Reformer* and excerpts from the unpublished "Ronald and Helen," started in 1861 and finished in 1864. The only new poems printed were the slight and unimportant "The Nightingale That Was Not Heard," "Creeds and Men," and "To Anna Linden," and the verse for the two Cope's "Christmas Cards."

But in addition to these bits, Thomson wrote a rough first draft of another poem, "I Had a Love." [75] Except for a few scattered passages the work is of little literary merit and echoes strongly many of his earlier works, both prose and poetry. Nevertheless it has biographical value as the major expression of Thomson's emotions and thoughts of these years.

The poem breaks into three parts. The first, reminiscent

---

[75] Because Thomson never revised the poem, he requested shortly before his death that it never be printed. Nevertheless Salt quoted freely from the work and Dobell, on pp. 36–38 of *The Laureate of Pessimism,* not only quoted but also offered a detailed summary, following the poem line by line and using much of Thomson's phraseology. Because the whole poem is not easily available, I have quoted more extensively than I would have done otherwise, but I have made it a point to use only material not quoted by Salt or Dobell.

of the desert scene in "The City," tells that after the death of
his Love, the narrator had wandered in the Desert of Despair,
where his heart had fed on its own poisoned flesh and his soul
drunk of its own bitter blood. The second part contains the
idea of the Proem of "The City," that in the expression of
thoughts and emotions are solace and satisfaction. The third
part also recalls "The City," not merely because of the
ideas but also, in places, because of its strength of expression.
One such passage, a denial of personal immortality and the
importance of the human race, might well be mistaken for
a section of "The City," both for its contents and the tone
and for its form, the six-line stanza rhyming *ababcc:*

> Now, when I see that we are all resolved
>     Into the Universe
> Whence so mysteriously we were evolved;
>     That all our parts disperse
> Never to build our very selves again,
> Though roses spring from roses, men from men.
>
> Now, when I see that all our little race
>     Must have its death as birth;
> Notes in infinities of Time and Space
>     Less during than our Earth,
> This many-insect-peopled drop of dew
> Exhaling in a moment from the view;
>
> Yea, now that I have learned by grievous thought
>     Something of Life and Death,
> And how the one is, like the other, naught,
>     Except for painful breath;
> And now that I have learnt with infinite toil
> To know myself, involved in such a coil.

Another such passage, which might also be inserted in "The City" without incongruity, expresses again the futility of life and the uselessness of life's pain:

> What profit from all life and lives on earth?
>     What good, what use, what aim?
> What compensation for the throes of birth
>     And death in all its frame,
> What consciousness life had ever paid its cost?
> From nothingness to nothingness—all lost!

New in the poem is one element, apparent throughout, Thomson's feeling that death was very near for him. Nowhere before had he expressed such a thought nor, as a matter of fact, did he express it later when death actually was close at hand.

>     And I am near the shore
> Of that Dead Sea where we find end of woes,
> Unconscious, oblivion, full repose.

The complete poem of twenty-five stanzas, one hundred fifty lines, was written in the three evenings of September 16, 17, and 18, 1876, three evenings during which Thomson's depression over his poetic sterility was replaced by a new hope, born of this sudden resurgence of his creative impulses. The diary entry for the first evening implies this hope: "Actually got writing verse again!" It is even more clearly seen in a postcript written on the fourth evening and attached to the poem when he copied it into the Green Book, where he entered all his rough drafts for future revision.[76]

---

[76] In addition, the following verses are included in the postscript:
> I do not hate a single man alive,
>     Some few I must disdain;
> I have loved heartily some four or five

Writing the foregoing lines, I have felt like a man making his will at the gates of Death, summing up life's scores and settling accounts when about to leave its inn. Yet I do not truly feel very near to Death, for with a seeming partial revival of the creative energies in thought and imagination, it is impossible to realize Death, even when absorbed by its somber fascination. It may be merely the throes of the new births that give the lethal illusion, for birth is so like death.

But the hope was short-lived. Thomson did not even attempt revision; perhaps he was convinced of the truth of his comment that the poem was "too hard and harsh in both conception and execution for attempt at polishing—far more truth than poetry in it"; more likely, I think, since it was no more hard and harsh than "The City," the "seeming revival of the creative energies" was a mere flash. But whatever the cause of his failure to revise, the creative impulses were gone; until November, 1881, he wrote no more poetry.[77]

Speculation concerning the cause of this sterility is profitable, for the facile explanation that Thomson, in his early and middle forties, was past his prime fails to consider the fact that the last year of his life, 1882, was second only to 1866 in amount of poetic production.[78] There are, however, other

---

And of these there remain
Just two, I think, for whom I would outface
Death gladly; for the one death and disgrace.

Who these friends might have been and the significance of the lines in relation to "I Had a Love" raise puzzling questions for which no satisfactory answers have ever been suggested.

[77] The single exception is an occasional piece done for the Secular Society, to be noted in the following chapter.

[78] A summary of Thomson's poetical output, though rough because of the lack of a few dates and questionableness of a few more, is significant

reasonable and more tenable explanations. In the first place, there are two contributing factors: after his return from Spain in late 1873, Thomson's health deteriorated rapidly; and from mid-1875, abasing poverty worried and harassed him and forced him to grind out journalistic articles unceasingly to provide himself with the barest of livings. Both sapped his mental energy and his physical strength to such an extent that poetry would have taken more than a normal amount of will to write. But more basic than these factors was, in my opinion, his emotional health. The rapid and marked decrease in the quantity of his poetry dates from 1867, just after he had moved from the Bradlaugh home into the heart of London and when the moods of hopelessness and despair began to dominate him. Such moods are usually emotionally devitalizing; they exercise a numbing, sometimes almost a paralyzing, influence. Substantiation of this theory that they were largely responsible for the long barren period is offered by the fact that in 1881, when Thomson left London and his almost constant depression, he began again to write poetry, though it is to be admitted that at the same time he left London he also left financial pressure. Stronger evidence, therefore, is a poem, written in 1882, "The Poet and His Muse," on the manuscript

---

in showing trends. In the decade of the 1850's, he wrote twenty-nine pieces, twenty-three of them in the last three years; in the 1860's, forty-eight; in the 1870's, sixteen, more than half of which were short epigrams; and in the three years of the 1880's before his death, sixteen. A division of these works according to the pattern used in this study runs thus: in the first period, including Thomson's army years, 1852–1862, he wrote thirty-seven items; in the second, during which he lived with the Bradlaughs, 1862–1866, thirty-one; in the third, twenty, of which approximately half were short epigrams; in the fourth, only five, all in 1877 and 1878; and in the last period, fifteen. The single year of highest productivity was 1866; the next was that of his death, 1882.

of which he scribbled, "Not true now, but true of seven song-less years." In this poem he himself assigned the reason for his failure to produce verse.

The poem begins with the plea that the Poet's Muse came to him again and

> . . . a little life and joy infuse
>    Into my brain and heart so weary now;
>  Into my heart so sad with emptiness
>
>              .       .       .
>
>  Into my brain so feeble and so listless,
>  Crushed down by burthens of dark thought resistless
> Of all our want and woe and unresulting strife.

In response to his appeal she comes, cold, bloodless, soulless, lightless, a phantom of his Muse, who is now dead; and she answers him:

> Lo, you have ravaged me with dolorous thought
> Until my brain was wholly overwrought,
>    Barren of flowers and fruit;
> Until my heart was bloodless for all passion,
> Until my trembling lips could no more fashion
> Sweet words to fit sweet airs of trembling lyre and lute.

The words and phrases that he chose—weary, sad, emptiness, feeble, listless, crushed, burthens, dark thoughts, dolorous thought, bloodless—are the words that belong with moods of depression. They are the words which to me explain Thomson's "seven songless years."

# CHAPTER V

# "The Drear Path"

## 1881~1882

THE last period of Thomson's life began in early 1881 when he went to Leicester to attend the opening of a new Secularist hall. At the ceremony, a poem was read which he had written for the occasion.[1] While in Leicester he met and quickly gained the friendship of J. W. Barrs and his sister, Miss Barrs, to whose home he returned early in June, after an interval in London, for a holiday of five and a half weeks. Four miles out of the city, the Barrs establishment, with its pleasant lawn, its neat kitchen garden, its cool green shrubs, and its meadow inviting the idler to leisurely rambles, was especially delightful to Thomson, coming thus to the country from his cramped quarters in London. On fair days the three friends went for drives and walks and picnics in the wooded countryside or

---

[1] This *Address on the Opening of the New Hall of the Leicester Secular Society,* written in what Thomson described as "colloquial rhyme," was delivered by Mrs. Theodore Wright four times during the course of the celebration; and after her first reading, copies were sold by members of the Society. The *Address* was well received. In addition to the Secular Society meetings, there were many social events (diary, March 5 through 9, 1881).

played lawn tennis. Evenings the men spent smoking and reading or chatting, often till two in the morning unless Thomson was able to withstand his host's "evil and powerfully contagious habit of sitting up" and retire at a more seasonable hour. In such environment Thomson's spirits rose; he began to feel better and the out-of-door exercise even dispelled his insomnia temporarily.[2]

In better physical and mental health and more stimulated to write than he had been for almost ten years, he returned late in July to London, where he at once began to work on the "Notes on the Structure of Shelley's Prometheus Unbound," which shortly appeared in the *Athenaeum,* and started the two Browning essays, considered in the preceding chapter, " 'The Ring and the Book' " and the "Notes on the Genius of Robert Browning." But three months later he went again to Leicester; he had not felt well in London and, after *Cope's* had ceased publication in January, 1881, he had had no regular employment to keep him there, so he was happy to respond to the Barrses' repeated invitations to return to them.[3] Thus by mid-November he was back with his warm-hearted friends. The Barrs encouraged him to work by providing a convenient place to write and, it is implied by Thomson's letters, attempted to build up his health. Moreover they set themselves the task of keeping liquor from him by seeing that there was none in the house and that he had no money with which to buy any. Yet with a cunning so uncharacteristic of his honest, straightforward nature that it shows more clearly than any-

---

[2] Letters to Bertram Dobell, June 21; to Miss Barrs, June 25; to Percy Holyoake, July 6, 1881; all quoted by Salt, *op. cit.,* pp. 160–163.

[3] Letter to Bertram Dobell, December 1, 1881, quoted by Salt, *op. cit.,* pp. 171–172.

thing else how disordered his mind had become, he occasionally managed to find a few pennies and slip away for a drink.[4]
On the whole, however, he was waging a good fight with the
help of the Barrses, and for a while there was hope that he
might win it.

Thomson immediately took advantage of the opportunity
to start writing. Some ten years earlier he had made notes
for "A Voice from the Nile"; [5] in November, 1881, he wrote
it, his last piece of philosophic verse. To the Nile, symbol of
unchanging, unending nature, man is the least comprehensible of all animals: he has neither the independence nor social
equality of the others; he is forever changing, first one race,
then another, gaining domination; and finally, he most in-
explicably created gods and demons, heaven and hell, which
also change. Such a concept was well suited to Thomson's
abilities, but he was unable at this time to handle it. The
development is uneven; the proportions are such that one feels
that he originally intended the poem to be nearer eight hundred lines than two, but that, the opening pages having
wearied him, he condensed his remaining ideas into a couple
of pages. Very possibly he found that, even in the new, ad-
vantageous environment, his strength was unequal to the
task of composing such a long poem.

In the same month, he wrote some stanzas addressed to
"H.A.B.," probably Miss Barrs, and in the next month,
December, a more important, longer work called "Richard
Forest's Midsummer Night," consisting of eleven lyrics of

---

[4] Information concerning this period was given by J. H. Barrs to Salt
on 1898, who, although he did not use it in his *Life,* communicated it to
Dobell. It is through the courtesy of Percy Dobell that I have had access
to the written account of these months.

[5] Salt, *op. cit.,* p. 239.

high quality. These are marked by several excellent descriptions which recall, because of the setting and mood, the best descriptive lyrics in "Ronald and Helen," written about nineteen years earlier. At the same time "Richard Forest" is reminiscent of "Sunday up the River," both in tone and in the presentation of a pair of young lovers. Its characters are more alive, however, than those of "Sunday up the River" and it therefore has more appeal.

Following "Richard Forest" came "At Belvoir," a pleasant narrative also about young lovers, "The Sleeper," and "A Modern Penelope." These four poems reintroduce into Thomson's writing a type of poetry he had dropped almost entirely during the fifteen years since, when living with the Bradlaughs on the edge of London, he had written "Sunday up the River," "Sunday at Hampstead," and the other Cockney poems. It can hardly be mere coincidence that again in the country, again a member of a family group, he immediately began once more to write light, gay verse. The parallel is so complete that one concludes that Thomson's "cheerful" poetry of both periods was the product of the country, of congenial companionship, and of the comforts of a home. And again one wonders if "The City of Dreadful Night" would ever have been written had Thomson remained in the pleasant surroundings of the Bradlaugh home instead of moving to London in 1866.

In January, Thomson went down to London and almost immediately became ill or, it is to be suspected, suffered an attack of dipsomania. By the first week in February he was trying to return to Leicester and the care of his friends, but he was so wretched that he was forced to ask for help in packing his clothes.[6] Back with the Barrs after an absence of three weeks, he again felt better and picked up his writing where he had left off. By the end of the month he had finished two poems, "The Poet and His Muse," a personal lyric to which I referred at some length in the previous chapter, and the longer "He Heard Her Sing," a strange poem, unlike anything he had ever written. The conception back of the poem may be loosely characterized as a glorification of abstract love in terms of music. The heart of the work is Thomson's impressionistic description of a song of love, a description which attempts to translate music into material imagery. It is first a tree, whose roots fill the sea, whose branches fill the sky; its leaves are the clouds, its silver fruit the stars. Yet the stars are the notes, the moon the voice of the song. Then it is a mighty crystal fountain, whose shaft is a column of light, whose spray is the clouds. The night is a shell for the music. Technically, the description amounts only to an expanded metaphor; but the subtlety with which Thomson worked it out, the effectiveness and beauty, the emotion, the feeling of spontaneity, and above all, the illusion of life with which he invested it, are absent in the dry term "expanded metaphor." The poem shows that in this poetic renascence his poetic impulses were fresh and strong, that he was capable even of innovations in technique.

The following month, March, Thomson wrote "Insomnia," one of his best poems. Yet in spite of its merits it is distressing reading, for it foretells with cruel clarity his impending collapse. Thomson was suffering not pain, but that which

---

[6] Letter to Percy Holyoake, February 6, 1881, quoted by Salt, *op. cit.*, p. 172.

is even harder to bear, chronic insomnia that eats into one's heart and mind until he is all but mad with fatigue and despair. The strength of feeling shows how horribly Thomson was racked in body and spirit. Worn out by a long succession of sleepless nights, he dreaded to go to bed lest the night ahead again be sleepless. Shutting his eyes firmly and simulating sleep, he saw before him a

> . . . black waste of ridge walls, hour by hour apart,
> Dividing deep ravines. . . .

Down the side of each he had to climb, slipping, falling; then cross the icy, swirling stream at the bottom, which threatened to sweep his tired legs from under him, and finally drag himself painfully up the other side, bruising his feet against the rocks and roots, losing his footing in the sliding sand, till at last he reached the top. And from the top, he saw another such ravine to be crossed. As he thus passed the night, an Hour stood sentinel at the head of his bed, an Hour which could not fly, for it could use its wings only when the sufferer slept. Finally, as light began to break over the cold, grey, foggy city, he rose abruptly, dressed feverishly, and, slipping out of his room as though terrified that the Hour might follow him, went into the street. There he reflected on his life, a dolorous series of defeats and black disasters. "Our poor vast petty life is one dark maze of dreams."

In "Insomnia," Thomson translated with even greater effectiveness than in "He Heard Her Sing" the intangible into the concrete. The reader is left knowing not merely with what the pain and agony might be compared, but what they actually were. He does not merely understand the agony that Thomson suffered; he has experienced the agony with him.

The poem is made powerful with the intensity of Thomson's suffering; and one is conscious that it is too great to be supported long.

With "Insomnia" the best of Thomson's poetry was written. In the next few weeks he wrote four more poems, none good, three very poor.[7] Occasional in nature, savoring of the early things he had scrawled off for the *National Reformer,* they show that his revived creative powers had died down; these were only embers. Thomson was burned out, creatively as well as physically. He had written some sixteen hundred lines in six months; he would write no more.

One more fact concerning the poetry of this last period of Thomson's work must be noted. Nearly two-thirds of it— and, excepting "Insomnia," the best two-thirds—is on the theme of love and clearly not on his old love for Matilda. It has been suggested that Thomson had fallen in love with Miss Barrs; in an article on Thomson in *The Free Thinker* in 1935, Victor B. Newburg stated, "At the time of his passing, the poet was engaged to Miss Barrs. . . . My source for this addition to the public knowledge of B.V. is my old and gifted friend and colleague, Vanoc II., of the *Sunday Referee,* himself a Leicester man, and probably the greatest living authority on B.V.'s life and works." Unquestionably, the "greatest living authority" at that date was Salt, and if it was he who supplied Newburg with the information, it is undoubtedly accurate, for Salt worked with the Barrs when writing his *Life* and enjoyed their confidence. Because, however, I have been unable to find any evidence which would identify Vanoc as Salt and because I can find in Thomson's

---

[7] "A Stranger," "The Old Story and the New Storey," "Law v. Gospel," and "Despotism Tempered by Dynamite."

letters, either those to the Barrs or those concerning them and their life when he was staying with them, no word nor implication which might substantiate the story, I cannot accept it.[8] On the other hand, I have no explanation for his preoccupation with the love theme.

In April Thomson once again evaded the kindly watchfulness of the Barrs and disappeared from their home. Some hours later he was found in a pub, hopelessly drunk. When he recovered, he readily agreed with the Barrs that he should return to London and remain there until the memory of the attack was less painful to all. Back in London he wrote the Barrs a quiet, dignified note, expressing his remorse for his actions and his gratitude for their kindness and bidding them good-by. The simplicity and sincerity of the note show the fineness of character that Thomson retained in his better moments even after he had become a psychopathic case, more frequently mad than sane. I quote it in full as one last picture of good before the horrible one that follows.

7 Huntley Street, Gower Street, W.C.<br>Friday, April 22, 1882.

Dear Mr. Barrs,—I scarcely know how to write you after my atrocious and disgusting return for the wonderful hospitality of yourself and Miss Barrs. I can only say that I was mad. In one fit of frenzy I have not only lost more than I yet know, and half murdered myself (were it not for my debts I sincerely wish it had been wholly), but justly alienated my best and firmest friends, old and new, both in London and Leicester.

---

[8] The Newburg article is so superficial that I am unwilling to accept his statements as authoritative unless further substantiated, however interesting they may be.

As, unfortunately for myself at least, I am left alive, it only remains for me to endeavor my utmost by hard and persistent struggling to repay my mere money debts, for my debts of kindness can never be repaid. If I fail, as very probably I shall fail, the failure will but irresistibly prove what I have long thoroughly believed, that for myself and others, I am much better dead than alive.

As apologies would be worse than useless, I will conclude by simply expressing my deep gratitude for your astonishing undeserved goodness to myself, and my best wishes for the welfare of you and yours.——In all sincerity,

James Thomson [9]

With this episode the story of Thomson's life ends; there remains only the story of his death, which his friends sincerely believed was his suicide, feeling that he consciously and willfully drank himself to death.[10] Psychiatrists whom I have consulted are agreed, however, that a dipsomaniac, although he may decide on self-destruction and even obtain the means therefor, will not, because of his weakened will, commit the act and that it is impossible for such a person to drink himself to death, a process involving purposefulness over a long period of time. It is, nevertheless, easy to understand the attitude of his friends. To commit suicide was in keeping with the courage Thomson had always displayed.

---

[9] Quoted by Salt, 1914 edition, pp. 137–138.

[10] The history of the six weeks is found in a series of letters exchanged by Thomson's London and Leicester friends, J. W. and H. H. Barrs and Percy Holyoake, dated March 20, April 17, 22, 24, May 9, 11, 12, 25, and 31, 1882. Copies of these are in the possession of Percy Dobell, who permitted me to read them.

Moreover it is known that the idea of suicide was in his mind during these weeks, for several times he threatened to destroy himself. And there is a hint of suicide in the fires which he started in the interior of buildings and from which he did not flee.

Up to this time a straight, sturdy, well-groomed man, Thomson now so lost his pride and dignity that he shuffled along the street in old, worn carpet slippers showing his bare feet. His curly brown hair and beard, streaked with grey, were ragged and unkempt; and his clothes, soiled with dirt from alley walls and the streets, were rumpled and creased from having been slept in. When a friend offered him a small loan to get a decent meal and a night's lodgings, he accepted it only for the purpose of treating the lender to a drink.[11]

The police, whom Thomson encountered almost daily during this period, recognized that he was mentally ill and more often obtained medical aid for him than arrested him. Finally, however, it became necessary to label him as incorrigible. A sympathetic magistrate, who knew the case and hoped to help Thomson through restraint, sentenced him, under an assumed name so that he might not have a prison record, to a fortnight in the prison hospital. His friends, who had hitherto provided bail whenever he was arrested, reluctantly agreed to try the experiment, but it was unsuccessful; released, Thomson continued to drink. During this entire period his friends did everything possible to help him, even working out a plan to send him to a sanatorium for inebriates at Liverpool; but he refused to go, and since they had no legal means of forcing

---

[11] W. Stewart Ross, in the *Agnostic Review*, April 6, 1889.

him, they were unable to put the scheme into execution. They were further hindered by the fact that often for days at a time they were unable to find him.

On June 1, Thomson went to the apartment of his friend, Philip Bourke Marston, where he put the blind man through a harrowing experience and then retired to the bedroom to lie down.[12] When William Sharp dropped in a few hours later and the distraught and helpless Marston sent him to see about their friend, he found that Thomson had suffered a severe hemorrhage. Shortly thereafter Herbert Clarke came in, and, after unavoidable delays, they finally got Thomson to the University College Hospital, that bleak building but a minute's walk from the rooms in which he had lived so many years.[13]

On the following day when Marston and Sharp visited him they found him confident of recovery, insisting that he would be out in three days if he had to come out in his coffin; the doctors, however, held no hope for his recovery. But Thomson was right. The next night, June 3, he died of exhaustion following severe intestinal hemorrhages. And on June 5,

---

[12] What the experience was, I do not know. Sharp, in *Papers Critical and Reminiscent,* vol. 3, mentions one but with good taste omits details. Frank Harris, however, in *Contemporary Portraits,* ser. 2, recounts with characteristic sensationalism a tale of Thomson's actions during an attack of delirium tremens. Ford Madox Ford, in *Reminiscences,* also tells a lurid story, similar in basic facts to the Harris story, of an "unnamed" poet so suffering; from the text one infers that he was writing of Thomson. But neither of these stories, nor even Sharp's brief reference, has been authenticated.

[13] In Salt's first edition of the *Life* he used the Sharp account of Thomson's death, but in the 1914 abridged edition he used the Herbert Clarke story. There are minor differences between the two, but the fundamental facts are the same. Clarke's account is, however, a little the fuller.

the third day, his body was removed from the hospital.[14]

He was buried June 8 in the grave of Austin Holyoake in Highgate Cemetery, that cemetery established so that those whose beliefs precluded their burial in consecrated ground might not be put in a potter's field. In his grave with him, Miss Scott, the housekeeper at his lodgings, who knew the little intimacies of his daily life better than his friends, placed a locket containing a yellow curl, a souvenir of Matilda cherished for twenty-nine years. An adaptation of the Secularist Burial Service, written years before by Austin Holyoake, was read by Theodore Wright.

Today in the cemetery, a few hundred yards down the hill from the graves of George Eliot, George Henry Lewes, Karl Marx, and George Jacob Holyoake, is Thomson's neglected grave, overgrown by grass and weeds, the stone all but hidden by a drooping, unpruned shrub. On the leaning headstone the lettering has been almost worn away by the water which

---

[14] It is probable that, if we knew Thomson's last words, we would find them significant as a last example of his strength of character. Sharp, in reviewing Salt's *Life* in the *Academy,* April 13, 1889, wrote, "I may add that the 'last words' of Thomson as given by Mr. Salt are perhaps a kindly but otherwise scarcely justifiable modification of those actually spoken." And Llewelyn Powys in *The Freeman,* September 6, 1922, in an article called "A Tragedy of Genius," wrote, "What, exactly, were Thomson's last words had never been divulged. It had been hinted that they were such as to cause even his friends to look askance." The significance, if there is one, lies in the fact that several times in his writings—in a "Jotting" in the *National Reformer,* in his review of Mill's *Essays,* in his essay on Rabelais—Thomson had expressed his impatience and annoyance with those pious people who, by twisting the last words of a well-known and avowed atheist, no matter how trivial, made it appear that on his deathbed he "saw the light," to use Thomson's own expression. Thomson, I am inclined to believe, uttered a dying speech of such a heretical nature that it could never be so misconstrued, that he could never be accused of facing death with less intellectual honesty than he had faced life.

drips from the shrub; one can trace with a finger more easily than read the words "James Thomson," carved two-thirds of the way down the stone, below the name and dates of Austin Holyoake.

# Bibliography

## I. WORKS OF JAMES THOMSON

### A. BOOKS AND PAMPHLETS

*Address on the Opening of the New Hall of the Leicester Secular Society* . . . *March 6, 1881.* No place, no date.

*Biographical and Critical Studies,* ed. Bertram Dobell. London: Reeves and Turner and Bertram Dobell, 1896.

*The City of Dreadful Night and Other Poems.* London: Reeves and Turner, 1880.

*A Commission of Inquiry on Royalty, Etc.* London: 1876.

*The Devil in the Church of England and The One Thing Needful.* London: "Secularist" Office, 1876.

*Essays and Phantasies.* London: Reeves and Turner, 1881.

*Essays, Dialogues and Thoughts of Giacomo Leopardi,* ed. Bertram Dobell. (New Universal Library.) London: George Routledge and Sons, Ltd., 1905.

*The Pilgrimage to Saint Nicotine.* Liverpool: Cope's Tobacco Plant, 1878.

*Poems, Essays, and Fragments,* ed. John M. Robertson. London: A. and H. B. Bonner, 1892.

*The Poetical Works of James Thomson (B.V.),* ed. Bertram Dobell. 2 vols. London: Reeves and Turner and Bertram Dobell, 1895.

*Satires and Profanities,* ed. G. W. Foote. London: Progressive Publishing Company, 1884.

*Selections from Original Contributions by James Thomson to "Cope's Tobacco Plant."* Liverpool: Cope's Tobacco Plant, 1889.

*Shelley, a Poem; with Other Writings Relating to Shelley, by the late James Thomson (B.V.): to which is added an Essay on the Poetry of William Blake by the same author.* London: Privately printed, 1884.

*The Story of a Famous Old Jewish Firm.* London: 1876.

*The Story of a Famous Old Jewish Firm and Other Pieces in Prose and Rime.* Imprinted for B.E. and W.L.S., 1883.

*James Thomson ("B.V.") on George Meredith.* London: Privately printed, 1909.

*Vane's Story, Weddah and Om-el-Bonain, and Other Poems.* London: Reeves and Turner, 1881.

*A Voice from the Nile and Other Poems,* ed. Bertram Dobell. London: Reeves and Turner, 1884.

*Walt Whitman: The Man and the Poet,* ed. Bertram Dobell. London: Bertram Dobell, 1910.

B. CONTRIBUTIONS TO PERIODICALS WITH NOTATION
OF FIRST APPEARANCE IN BOOKS

1. *The London Investigator*

1858

"Mr. Save-His-Soul-Alive, O!" February.

"Notes on Emerson," December. *(Poems, Essays, and Fragments)*

1859

"The King's Friends," February. *(Poems, Essays, and Fragments)*

[ 176 ]

"A Few Words about Burns," April. (*Poems, Essays, and Fragments;* poem from essay in *A Voice from the Nile and Other Poems* as "Robert Burns")

2. *Tait's Edinburgh Magazine*

### 1858

"The Fadeless Bower," July. (*Vane's Story and Other Poems*)

"Four Stages in a Life," October. (*Poetical Works,* vol. 2, as "Four Points in a Life")

### 1859

"A Festival of Life," April. (*A Voice from the Nile and Other Poems*)

"Tasso to Leonora," May. (*A Voice from the Nile and Other Poems*)

"The Cypress and the Roses," June. (*Vane's Story and Other Poems*)

"Withered Leaves," July. (*Vane's Story and Other Poems*)

"The Jolly Veterans," August. (*Vane's Story and Other Poems*)

"A Capstan Chorus," August. (*Vane's Story and Other Poems*)

"Bertram to the Most Noble and Beautiful Lady Geraldine," November. (*Vane's Story and Other Poems*)

"To Arabella Goddard," November. (*The City of Dreadful Night and Other Poems,* as "To a Pianist")

"A Happy Poet," December. (*A Voice from the Nile and Other Poems*)

### 1860

"The Purple Flower of the Heather," January. (*Poetical Works,* vol. 2)

"A Winter's Night," January. (*Poetical Works,* vol. 2)

"The Lord of the Castle of Indolence," March.  (*The City of Dreadful Night and Other Poems*)
"An Old Dream," June.  (*Poetical Works*, vol. 2)
3. *National Reformer*

### 1860

"A Letter addressed to the Editor, on Shelley's Religious Opinions," August 26.  (*Shelley, a Poem; with Other Writings Relating to Shelley*, as "Shelley's Religious Opinions")
"Scrap Book Leaves," Nos. 1 and 2, September 1 and 22.
"Shelley," December 22.  (*Shelley, a Poem; with Other Writings Relating to Shelley*)

### 1861

"The Dead Year," January 6.  (*Poems, Essays, and Fragments*)

### 1862

"The Established Church," November 15.  (*Satires and Profanities*)
"Heresy," November 22.  (*The City of Dreadful Night and Other Poems*, as "A Recusant")
"Elizabeth Barrett Browning," November 29.  (*The City of Dreadful Night and Other Poems*, as "E. B. B.")
"The Mountain Voice," from Heine, December 6.  (*The City of Dreadful Night and Other Poems*)
"The Life of Moses, by J. Lolsky," a review, December 13.
"Songs from Heine," December 20.
"The Greek Gods," from Heine, December 27.  (*Poems, Essays, and Fragments*)

### 1863

"The Meaning of History, by F. Harrison," a review, January 3.

"To the Youngest of Our Ladies of Death," February 28. (*The City of Dreadful Night and Other Poems,* as "To Our Ladies of Death")

1864

"Thomas Cooper's Argument for the Existence of Deity," February 13. (*Poems, Essays, and Fragments,* as "On a Debate Between Mr. Bradlaugh and Mr. Thomas Cooper on the Existence of God")

"The Good God," from Béranger, July 11. (*Poems, Essays, and Fragments*)

"Poems and Songs, by J. M. Peacock," a review, November 19.

1865

"The Athanasian Creed," January 1. (*Satires and Profanities*)

"Body and Soul," from Heine, February 5. (*The City of Dreadful Night and Other Poems*)

"The Death of the Devil," from Béranger, March 26. (*Poems, Essays, and Fragments*)

"The Almighty Devil," July 30.

"Mr. Kingsley's Convertites," September 24. (*Satires and Profanities*)

"Bumble, Bumbledom, Bumbleism," October 29 and November 5. (*Essays and Phantasies*)

"Per Contra: The Poet, High Art, Genius," November 12 and 19. (*Essays and Phantasies*)

"An Evening with Spenser," November 26. (*Essays and Phantasies*)

"Mr. Gladstone's Edinburgh Address," December 10.

"Virtue and Vice," December 17. (*The City of Dreadful Night and Other Poems*)

"The Story of a Famous Old Firm," December 24 and 31. (*The Story of a Famous Old Jewish Firm*)

[ 179 ]

1866

"Christmas Eve in the Upper Circles," January 7. (*Satires and Profanities*)

"The Poems of William Blake," January 14, 21, and 28, February 4. (*Poems, Essays, and Fragments;* poem from essay in *A Voice from the Nile and Other Poems* as "William Blake")

"Four Scraps from Heine," February 11.

"Open Secret Societies," February 18 and 25, March 4. (*Essays and Phantasies*)

"Jesus: as God; as Man," March 18. (*Satires and Profanities*)

"The Polish Insurgent," March 18. (*The City of Dreadful Night and Other Poems*)

"A Timely Prayer," March 18. (*Poems, Essays, and Fragments*)

"Vane's Story," May 13 and 27, June 3 and 10. (*Vane's Story and Other Poems*)

"Liberty and Necessity," May 20. (*Essays and Phantasies*)

"Goethe's Israel in the Wilderness," June 17 and 24, July 1 and 8.

"Who Killed Moses?" July 15. (*Poems, Essays, and Fragments*)

"Sunday at Hampstead," July 15 and 22. (*The City of Dreadful Night and Other Poems*)

"The One Thing Needful," August 5. (*Satires and Profanities*)

"Suggested from Southampton," September 2. (*Poems, Essays, and Fragments*)

"Sayings of Sigvat," September 30, October 14. (*Essays and Phantasies*)

"Polycrates on Waterloo Bridge," October 14. (*Vane's Story and Other Poems*)

"A Word for Xantippe," October 21. (*Essays and Phantasies*)

"Sympathy," October 28, November 18 and 25. (*Essays and Phantasies*)

"Versicles," November 25. (*Poems, Essays, and Fragments*)

"The Swinburne Controversy," December 23. (*Satires and Profanities*)

1867

"Life's Hebe," January 13. (*The City of Dreadful Night and Other Poems*)

"Philosophy," January 20. (*The City of Dreadful Night and Other Poems*)

"*The Saturday Review* on Mr. Bright's edition of Mr. Bright," February 3. (*Poems, Essays, and Fragments*)

"Giordano Bruno," February 10 and 24, March 3.

"Art," February 17. (*The City of Dreadful Night and Other Poems*)

"A Walk Abroad," April 21. (*Essays and Phantasies*)

"*The Saturday Review* and the *National Reformer*," April 28 and May 5. (Selection in *Satires and Profanities* as "A Word on Blasphemy")

"Heine on Kant," May 19.

"Heine on Spinoza," May 26, June 2.

"Heine on an Illustrious Exile with Something about Whales," June 9 and 16. (*Satires and Profanities*)

"The Naked Goddess," June 23. (*The City of Dreadful Night and Other Poems*)

"The Gift for our Lord the King," July 7. (*The City of Dreadful Night and Other Poems*, as "L'Ancien Régime; or, The Good Old Rule")

"A Lady of Sorrow," July 14, 21, and 28, August 4, 11, 18, and 24, September 1. (*Essays and Phantasies*)

"They Chanted," August 18. (*A Voice from the Nile and Other Poems,* as section ii of Part III of "The Doom of a City")

"Day," August 25. (*Vane's Story and Other Poems*)

"Night," August 25. (*Vane's Story and Other Poems*)

"A Requiem," September 1. (*Vane's Story and Other Poems*)

"The Pan Anglican-Synod," October 13. (*Poems, Essays, and Fragments*)

"Copernicus: a Dialogue," from Leopardi, November 3 and 10. (*Essays, Dialogues and Thoughts of Leopardi,* as "Copernicus")

"Europe's Rouge et Noir," November 24. (*Vane's Story and Other Poems*)

"Dialogue between a Natural Philosopher and a Metaphysician," from Leopardi, December 1. (*Essays, Dialogues and Thoughts of Leopardi*)

"Dialogue of Timander and Eleander," from Leopardi, December 8 and 15. (*Essays, Dialogues and Thoughts of Leopardi*)

"Dialogue between Nature and the Soul," from Leopardi, December 29. (*Essays, Dialogues and Thoughts of Leopardi*)

## 1868

"Dialogue of Christopher Columbus and Peter Gutierrez," from Leopardi, January 5. (*Essays, Dialogues and Thoughts of Leopardi*)

"Two Lovers," January 5. (*Vane's Story and Other Poems*)

"Dialogue between Frederic Ruysch and his Mummies," from Leopardi, January 26. (*Essays, Dialogues and Thoughts of Leopardi*)

"A German Village School," January 26.

# BIBLIOGRAPHY

"Dialogue between Tristan and a Friend," from Leopardi, February 6 and 9. (*Essays, Dialogues and Thoughts of Leopardi*)

"Dialogue between a Vendor of Almanacs and a Passer-by," from Leopardi, March 15. (*Essays, Dialogues and Thoughts of Leopardi*)

"In Praise of Birds," from Leopardi, March 22. (*Essays, Dialogues and Thoughts of Leopardi*)

"Dialogue of Plotinus and Porphyry," from Leopardi, April 5 and 12. (*Essays, Dialogues and Thoughts of Leopardi*)

"Comparison of the Last Words of Brutus the Younger, and Theophrastus," from Leopardi, May 3 and 17. (*Essays, Dialogues and Thoughts of Leopardi*)

"Selection from the Thoughts of Leopardi," May 31 and June 7. (*Essays, Dialogues and Thoughts of Leopardi, included in "Thoughts"*)

## 1869

"*The Pilgrim and the Shrine,* and its Critics," August 29.

## 1869–1870

"Leopardi," October 3, 10, and 17, November 7, 21, and 28, December 12, 1869; January 2, 9, and 16, February 6, 1870. (*Essays, Dialogues, and Thoughts of Leopardi,* as the first part of the "Memoir of Leopardi")

## 1870

"Paul Louis Courier," July 31, August 7 and 14.

"Prometheus," from Goethe, July 31. (*Vane's Story and Other Poems*)

"How the Bible Warns against Authorship," August 21. (*Poems, Essays, and Fragments*)

"Jottings," September 4.

[ 183 ]

"How Heine Forewarned France," September 11.   (*Poems, Essays, and Fragments*)

"Commission of Inquiry as to Complaints against Royalty," September 18.   (*A Commission of Inquiry on Royalty, Etc.*)

"Paul Louis Courier on the Land Question," October 9.

"Paul Louis Courier on the Character of the People," October 16.

"Marcus Aurelius Antonius," October 23 and 30, November 6.

"The Assassination of Paul Louis Courier," October 30.

"Our Visit to Aberdeen," November 6 and 13.

"Cowper's Task (New Version)," November 13.

"Hints for Freethought Novels," November 20.

"A Bible Lesson on Monarchy," November 27.   (*Satires and Profanities*)

"Feuerbach's Essence of Christianity," December 4.

"Infidelity in the United States," December 11.

"With the Christian World," December 18.

1871

"International Socialism in Spain," January 1.

"The Divan of Goethe," January 22.   (Selection in *Vane's Story and Other Poems* as "From the 'West Östlicher Divan' "; complete in *Poems, Essays, and Fragments*)

"Strange News for the Secularists," January 22.

"Atheism in Spain," February 5.

"Anastasius," February 12 and 19.

"Association for Intercessory Prayer," February 26.

"Moxon's Cheap Edition of Shelley's Poems," March 12.   (*Shelley, a Poem; with Other Writings Relating to Shelley*)

"In Exitu Israel," March 19.   (*Poems, Essays, and Fragments*)

"Change for a Bad Napoleon," March 19.

"Insults to the Church in Spain," April 2.

"Poor Indeed!" April 9. (*Poems, Essays, and Fragments*)

"The Successors Who Do Not Succeed," April 16. (*Poems, Essays, and Fragments*)

"Bless Thee! Thou Art Translated," April 23. (*Poems, Essays, and Fragments*)

"Cross Lines from Goethe," April 23. (*Poems, Essays, and Fragments*)

"Another Spanish Atheistic Periodical," April 30.

"We Croak," May 7. (*Poems, Essays, and Fragments*)

"In a Christian Churchyard," May 7. (*Poems, Essays, and Fragments*)

"Proposals for the Speedy Extinction of Evil and Misery," August 27, September 3, 10, 17, and 24, October 8 and 22, November 5 and 12. (*Essays and Phantasies*)

## 1871–1872

"Weddah and Om-el-Bonain," November 19, December 3 and 24, 1871; January 21 and 28, 1872. (*Vane's Story and Other Poems*)

## 1872

"Our Congratulations on the Recovery of His Royal Highness," January 28. (*Poems, Essays, and Fragments*)

"Pathetic Epitaph," January 28. (*Poems, Essays, and Fragments*)

"A Song of Sighing," April 28. (*Vane's Story and Other Poems*)

"In the Room," May 19. (*The City of Dreadful Night and Other Poems*)

"Modern Miracles," October 27.

## 1873

"Religion in the Rocky Mountains," March 30, April 13. (*Satires and Profanities*)

JAMES THOMSON (B.V.)

## 1874

"The City of Dreadful Night," March 22, April 12 and 26,
May 17. (*The City of Dreadful Night and Other Poems*)
"The Funeral of Mr. Austin Holyoake," April 26.
"Jottings," July 5, 12, 19, and 26, August 2, 16, 23, and 30,
September 6, 13, 20, and 27, November 1, 8, 15, 22, and
29, December 6, 13, and 20.
"A National Reformer in the Dog Days," July 12 and 19.
(*Essays and Phantasies*)
"Walt Whitman," July 26, August 2, 9, 16, 23, and 30,
September 6. (*Poems, Essays, and Fragments*)
"Uhland in English," September 13 and 20.
"Bishop Alford on Professor Tyndall," September 27.
"Extra-Experimental Beliefs," October 11.
"Jesus Christ, Our Great Exemplar," October 25.
"The *Daily News*," November 1. (*Satires and Profanities*)
"John Stuart Mill on Religion," November 8, 15, 22, and
29, December 6, 13, 20, and 27.

## 1875

"Henri Beyle (De Stendhal)," January 31, February 7 and 14.
"Jottings," January 31, February 7, 14, 21, and 28, March 7
and 14, April 4 and 25, May 2.
"Raffaele Sanzio," February 28.
"Great Christ is Dead," March 14. (*Satires and Profanities*)
"The Sankey Hymns," April 25.
"Archbishop of Canterbury on Fallacies of Unbelief," May 2.
"Mr. Moody's Addresses," May 16.
"A Popular Sermon," May 23.
"Some May Meeting Figures," May 30.
"Some May Meeting Speeches," June 6.
"Debate between Mr. C. Watts and Mr. T. B. Woffendale,"
June 13 and 20.

1891

"Selections from the Manuscript Books of 'B.V.,' " April 19
and 26, May 3, 10, 17, and 24, June 7 and 14, July 5,
12, and 19, August 23 and 30.    (Some in *Poems, Essays,
and Fragments* as "On Suicide" and "Fragments")

4. *The Secularist*

1876

"Secularism and the Bible," January 1.

"By the Sea," part I, January 1.    (*A Voice from the Nile;
Poetical Works,* vol. 2, as part of "Ronald and Helen")

"Reverberations," January 1.

"By the Sea," part II, January 8.    (*A Voice from the Nile;
Poetical Works,* vol. 2, as part of "Ronald and Helen")

"Whitman and Swinburne," January 8.

"Heinrich Heine," January 8, 15, 22, and 29, February 5 and
12.

"By the Sea," parts III and IV, January 15.    (*A Voice from
the Nile; Poetical Works,* vol. 2, as part of "Ronald and
Helen")

"By the Sea," part V, January 22.    (*A Voice from the Nile;
Poetical Works,* vol. 2, as part of "Ronald and Helen")

"Where?" from Heine, January 29.    (*The City of Dreadful
Night and Other Poems*)

"The Mountain Voice," from Heine, February 5.    (*The
City of Dreadful Night and Other Poems*)

"The Pilgrimage to Kevlaar," from Heine, February 12.
(*The City of Dreadful Night and Other Poems*)

"Arthur Schopenhauer," a review, February 19 and 26, March
11.

Poems from Heine, February 19 and 26, March 4 and 11.

"The Devil in the Church of England," February 26 and
March 4.    (*Satires and Profanities*)

"Carlist Reminiscences," March 11, 18, and 25, April 1.

"Goblin Market, The Prince's Progress, and Other Poems, by Christina G. Rossetti," a review, March 25.

"A Great Modern Astrologer," April 1.

"Dr. Kenealy in a New Character," April 8.

"The Secular Song and Hymn Book, edited by Annie Besant," a review, April 8.

"Mr. Matthew Arnold on the Church of England," April 8.

"Renan's Memories of his Childhood," April 15.

"Religion in Japan," April 22.

"Correspondence," April 22.

Three poems from Heine, April 29.

" 'The Bugbears of Infidelity' at Perth," May 6.

"Among the Christians," May 6.

"On the Worth of Metaphysical Systems," May 13.  (*Essays and Phantasies*)

Two poems from Heine, May 13.

"Correspondence (Mr. G. J. Holyoake on Party Unity)," May 13.

"The Burial Question in the House of Lords," May 20.

"Don Giovanni at Covent Garden," May 20.  (*Poetical Works,* vol. 1)

"The Life of Jonathan Swift, by John Forster," May 20.  (*Essays and Phantasies,* as "A Note on Forster's Life of Swift")

"The *Standard* on the Whigs and the Church," May 27.

"The Three that Shall Be One," June 3.  (*The City of Dreadful Night and Other Poems*)

"Beauchamp's Career," a review, June 3.  (A portion in *Essays and Phantasies,* as "A Note on George Meredith [on the Occasion of 'Beauchamp's Career']"; complete in *James Thomson ["B.V."] on George Meredith*)

"A Few Words on the System of Spinoza," June 10.  (*Essays and Phantasies*)

[ 188 ]

"The Leeds Conferences," June 17.

Poem from Heine, June 24.

"William Godwin: his Friends and Contemporaries, by C. Kegan Paul," a review, June 24, July 1 and 8.

"Seen Thrice: A London Study," July 8 and 15.

"The Bishop of London's Fund," July 15.

"Mr. Foote at the London Hall of Science," July 15.

"Christian Evidences, Popular and Critical," July 22 and 29.

"Indolence: a Moral Essay," July 22 and 29, August 5. (*Essays and Phantasies*)

"The Resurrection and Ascension of Jesus," August 5. (*Satires and Profanities*)

"Questions," from Heine, August 5. (*The City of Dreadful Night and Other Poems*)

"Some Muslim Laws and Beliefs," August 12 and 19. (*Satires and Profanities*)

"Shameless, Kew Gardens," August 12. (*Vane's Story and Other Poems*)

"Low Life," August 19. (*A Voice from the Nile and Other Poems*)

"Stray Thoughts," August 26.

"Among the Christians," August 26.

"The *Christian World* and the *Secularist* again," September 9. (*Satires and Profanities,* as "The *Christian World* and the *Secularist*")

"Pacchiarotto, by Robert Browning," September 9. (*Biographical and Critical Studies,* as "Browning's 'Pacchiarotto'")

"The Loreley," from Heine, September 9. (*The City of Dreadful Night and Other Poems*)

"Conversions Sudden and Gradual," September 16.

"The Easter Questions," September 16.

"Correspondence: 'Mr. G. J. Holyoake's Libels,' " September 16.

"On the Duty of Converts to Freethought," September 23.

"The London School Board Elections," September 30.

"The *Cornhill Magazine* on Leopardi," September 30.

Poem from Heine, September 30.

"La Tentation de Saint Antoine par Gustave Flaubert," September 30, October 7, 21, and 28, November 4.

"The Primate on the Church and the World," October 7. (*Satires and Profanities*)

"The *Daily News* on Materialism," October 7.

Poems from Heine, October 14 and November 4.

"Spiritism in the Police Court," November 11. (*Satires and Profanities*)

"The Huddersfield Prosecution of a 'Medium,' " November 18.

"The London School Board Elections," December 9.

"An Inspired Critic on Shelley," December 9. (*Shelley, a Poem; With Other Writings Relating to Shelley*)

"Note of an English Republican on the Muscovite Crusade, by A. C. Swinburne," December 30.

## 1877

"Our Obstructions," January 6. (*Satires and Profanities*)

"Among the Christians," January 6.

"The Works of Francis Rabelais," a review, January 6.

"In Our Forest of the Past," February 17. (*Essays and Phantasies*)

"Song, 'The Nightingale was not yet heard,' " February 17. (*A Voice from the Nile and Other Poems*, as "Song")

"Principal Tulloch on Personal Immortality," February 24. (*Satires and Profanities*)

"Professor Martineau and the Reverend H. H. Dobney on Prayer," March 3.

"The Bi-centenary of Spinoza, M. Renan's Address," March 10.

"The Discourses of Epictetus, translated by G. Long," a review, April 14 and 21, May 5 and 12.    (*Essays, Dialogues and Thoughts of Leopardi*)

5. *Secular Review and Secularist*

1877

"Trois Contes, par Gustave Flaubert," a review, July 21.

6. *Cope's Tobacco Plant*

(Meager excerpts from many of the following were printed in *Selections from James Thomson's Contributions to "Cope's Tobacco Plant."* Because these are very brief, notation of first appearance of an article in a book is made to the first book which gives a complete reprint.)

"Stray Whiffs from an Old Smoker," September, 1875.

"Charles Baudelaire on Hasheesh," October, 1875.

"Theophile Gautier as Hasheesh-Eater," November, 1875.

"A French Novel: Un Homme Serieux, by Charles de Bernard," a review, December, 1875.

"The Fair of St. Sylvester," January, 1876.    (*Essays and Phantasies*)

"Saint Amant," February, March, April, 1876.    (*Biographical and Critical Studies*)

"*Beauchamp's Career*," June, 1876.    (*James Thomson [B.V.] on George Meredith*)

"Rabelais," June, July, August, October, 1876.    (*James Thomson [B.V.] on George Meredith*)

"Ben Jonson," November, December, 1876, January, February, March, May, June, August, September, October, November, December, 1877, January, March, 1878.    (*Biographical and Critical Studies*)

"Rubáiyát of Omar Khayyám," March, 1877.

"To Anna Linden," January, 1878.

"John Wilson and the 'Noctes Ambrosianae,' " April, 1878, May, 1879.

"Tobacco Smuggling in the Last Generation," May, June, July, August, September, October, November, 1878.

"The Tobacco Duties," December, 1878, January, March, 1879.

" 'Social Notes' on Tobacco," January, 1879.

"Tobacco at the Opera," February, 1879.

"Tobacco Legislation in the Three Kingdoms," March, April, September, November, December, 1879, January, March, April, May, June, August, September, November, 1880.

"An Old New Book (*The Ordeal of Richard Feverel,*—a memorable critique)," May, 1879. (*James Thomson [B.V.] on George Meredith*)

"James Hogg, the Ettrick Shepherd," August, September, October, 1879. (*Biographical and Critical Studies*)

"George Meredith's New Work (*The Egoist*)," January, 1880. (*James Thomson [B.V.] on George Meredith*)

"Walt Whitman," May, June, August, September, December, 1880. (*Walt Whitman*)

"A Sergeant's Mess Song," November, 1880. (*Poems, Essays, and Fragments*)

7. *The Liberal*

1879

"In the Valley of Humiliation," January.

"Two Leaves of a Fadeless Rose of Love," January. (*Poetical Works,* vol. 2, as part of "Ronald and Helen")

"Professor Huxley on Hume," March.

Two Poems from Heine, May.

"Meeting Again," June. (*Vane's Story and Other Poems*)

"The Lover's Return," July. (*Poetical Works,* vol. 2, as part of "Ronald and Helen")

"A Strange Book," September, October, November, December.    (*Biographical and Critical Studies*)
8. *Progress*

### 1884

"A Note on Shelley," February.    (*Shelley, a Poem; with Other Writings Relating to Shelley*)
"Bill Jones on Prayer," August.    (*Poetical Works*, vol. 1)
"A Real Vision of Sin," November.    (*Poetical Works*, vol. 2)
"A Graveyard," December.

### 1885

"Supplement to the Inferno," February.    (*Poetical Works*, vol. 1)

### 1886

"Siren's Song," March.    (*Poetical Works*, vol. 2)

### 1887

"Sarpolus of Mardon," February, March, April, May, June.
"Aquatics (Kew)," November.
9. *Daily Telegraph*
"Middle Class Education," July 19, 1864.
10. *Fraser's Magazine*
"Sunday up the River," October, 1869.    (*The City of Dreadful Night and Other Poems*)
11. *National Secular Society's Almanac*
"Notes on Religious Matters," 1872.
"Some Anecdotes of Rabelais," 1876.
12. *Fortnightly Review*
"The Deliverer," November, 1881.    (*A Voice from the Nile and Other Poems*)
"A Voice from the Nile," July, 1882.    (*A Voice from the Nile and Other Poems*)

*"Proem,"* February, 1892.  (*Poems, Essays, and Fragments*)

13. *Athenaeum*

"Notes on the Structure of Shelley's Prometheus Unbound," September 17 and 24, October 8, November 5 and 19, 1881.  (*Shelley, a Poem; with Other Writings Relating to Shelley*)

14. *Gentleman's Magazine*

" 'The Ring and the Book,' " December, 1881.  (*Biographical and Critical Studies*)

15. *Weekly Dispatch*

### 1882

"Law v. Gospel," March 26.  (*A Voice from the Nile and Other Poems*)

"The Old Story and the New Storey," April 2.  (*A Voice from the Nile and Other Poems*)

"The Closure," April 30.

"Despotism Tempered by Dynamite," June 4.  (*A Voice from the Nile and Other Poems*)

16. *Browning Society's Transactions,* part I, 1882

"Notes on the Genius of Robert Browning."  (*Biographical and Critical Studies*)

### C. MANUSCRIPT MATERIAL

Thomson diaries of 1874, 1876, 1877, 1878, 1879, 1880, and 1881.

Dobell's notebook of unprinted poems, copied by him from Thomson's manuscripts, including the following:

> "Hymns to the Night," from Novalis
> "To My Sister"
> "The Approach to St. Paul's"
> "Poems to a Purple Flower"
> "Soldier Song"

## BIBLIOGRAPHY

"If I am Spared"
"Once in a Saintly Passion"
"A Slight Mistake"
"Lines" (I Had a Love)
"Two Impromptus"
Translations from Heine (prefaced by
    Thomson's theory of translation)
"The Star and Garter"
"Miscellanies"
First study of a passage from "The Doom of a City"
"Dürer's 'Melencholia,' " a first study of section xxi
    of "The City of Dreadful Night"


## II. BIOGRAPHICAL, CRITICAL, AND
## GENERAL

"B.E." "Introduction" to *The Story of a Famous Old Jewish Firm and Other Pieces in Prose and Rime*. Imprinted for B.E. and W.L.S., 1883.

Benton, Joel. "A New English Poet," *Appleton's Journal*, May, 1881.

Black, G. A. "James Thomson, His Translation of Heine," *Modern Language Review*, January, 1936.

Blunden, Edmund. "Introduction" to *The City of Dreadful Night and Other Poems*. New York: Methuen and Co., 1932.

Bonner, Hypatia Bradlaugh. *Charles Bradlaugh*. 2 vols. London: T. Fisher Unwin, 1895.

———. "Childish Recollections of James Thomson," *Our Corner*, August, 1886.

"Bysshe Vanolis," *London Times Literary Supplement*, June 9, 1932.

Carlyle, Thomas. *Reminiscences,* ed. J. A. Froude. New York: Charles Scribner's Sons, 1881.

Cavazza, E. "Introduction" to *The City of Dreadful Night.* Portland, Maine: Thomas Mosher, 1892.

Cazamian, Louis. *Etudes de psychologies litteraire.* Lausanne and Paris: Librairie Payot et Cie., 1913.

Church, R. "Pale Melancholy," *Spectator,* October 13, 1928.

"The City of Dreadful Night," a review, *Academy,* June 6, 1874.

"The City of Dreadful Night," a review, *Athenaeum,* May 1, 1880.

"The City of Dreadful Night" and "Vane's Story," a review, *London Quarterly Review,* April, 1881.

Dobell, Bertram. "Introduction" to *Essays, Dialogues and Thoughts of Giacomo Leopardi.* London: George Routledge and Sons, Ltd., n.d.

——. "Introduction" to *Walt Whitman: The Man and the Poet.* London: Bertram Dobell, 1910.

——. *The Laureate of Pessimism.* London: Bertram Dobell, 1910.

——. "Memoir" in *The Poetical Works of James Thomson (B.V.)* 2 vols. London: Reeves and Turner and Bertram Dobell, 1895.

——. "Memoir" in *A Voice from the Nile and Other Poems.* London: Reeves and Turner, 1884.

——. "Preface" to *The City of Dreadful Night and Other Poems.* London: Bertram Dobell, 1899.

——. "Preface" to *Shelley, a Poem; with Other Writings Relating to Shelley, by the late James Thomson (B.V.).* London: Privately printed, 1884.

——, and Wheeler, J. M. "Bibliography" in *The City of Dreadful Night.* Portland, Maine: Thomas Mosher, 1892.

Drummond, Andrew L. *Edward Irving and His Circle.* London: James Clarke and Co., Ltd., n.d.

Flaws, G. G. "James Thomson, a Study," *Secular Review,* June 24 and July 1, 1882.

Foote, G. W. "James Thomson," *National Reformer,* March 31, April 7, 14, and 21, 1889.

——. "James Thomson. I. The Man," *Progress,* April, 1884.

——. "James Thomson. II. The Poet," *Progress,* June, 1884.

——. "Preface" to *Satires and Profanities.* London: Progressive Publishing Co., 1884.

Ford, Ford Madox. *Memories and Impressions.* London and New York: Harper Bros., 1911.

Gerould, G. H. "Introduction" to *Poems of James Thomson "B.V."* New York: Henry Holt and Co., 1927.

Gilmour, J. P. (ed.). *Champion of Liberty: Charles Bradlaugh.* London: C. A. Watts and Co., Ltd. and The Pioneer Press, 1933.

*The Glory That Was Gold.* Denver: The Central City Opera House Association of the University of Denver, 1938.

Harris, Frank. *Contemporary Portraits.* (Ser. 2.) New York: Privately printed, 1919.

——. *My Life.* Privately printed, 1927.

Hillier, Arthur. "James Thomson," *Dublin University Review,* December, 1885.

Hoffman, H. "An Angel in the City of Dreadful Night," *Sewanee Review,* July, 1924.

Hoyt, A. S. *Spiritual Message of Modern English Poetry.* New York: Macmillan Co., 1924.

"James Thomson, (B.V.)," *Saturday Review,* February 16, 1895.

"James Thomson, (B.V.)," *Academy,* December 3, 1898.

Jordan, David Starr. *The Philosophy of Hope.* New York and San Francisco: Paul Elder and Co., 1902.

Lewin, Walter. "Introduction" to *Selections from Original Contributions by James Thomson to "Cope's Tobacco Plant."* Liverpool: Cope's Tobacco Plant, 1889.

Maccall, William. *A Nirvana Trilogy.* London: Watts and Co., 1886.

Marks, Jeannette. *Genius and Disaster.* New York: Adelphi Co., 1926.

Marston, P. B. "James Thomson" in *The English Poets,* ed. T. H. Ward. Students' ed. New York: Macmillan Co., 1880. Vol. IV.

———. Obituary notice, *Athenaeum,* June 10, 1882.

Meeker, James Edward. *The Life and Poetry of James Thomson (B.V.).* New Haven: Yale University Press, 1917.

Meredith, George. *Letters,* ed. W. W. Meredith. 2 vols. New York: Charles Scribner's Sons, 1912.

More, Paul E. *Shelburne Essays.* (Ser. 5.) New York: G. P. Putnam's Sons, 1908.

———. "Sketch and Works of James Thomson," *Nation,* December 26, 1907.

Newburg, Victor. "James Thomson," *The Free Thinker,* November 18 and 25, December 2, 1934.

Noel, Roden. "James Thomson" in *The Poets and Poetry of the Century,* ed. A. H. Miles. London: Hutchinson and Co., 1892. Vol. V.

Peyre, Henri. "Les Sources du pessimisme de Thomson," *Revue Anglo-Americaine,* December, 1924, and February, 1925.

Powys, Llewelyn. "A Tragedy of Genius," *The Freeman,* September 6, 1922.

Robertson, John M. "Preface" to *Poems, Essays, and Fragments.* London: A. and H. B. Bonner, 1892.

Rossetti, William M. *Some Reminiscences.* 2 vols. London: Brown Langham and Co., Ltd., 1906.

Saintsbury, George. "The City of Dreadful Night," a review, *Academy,* June 12, 1880.

Salt, Henry S. *Company I Have Kept.* London: George Allen and Unwin, Ltd., 1930.

———. "Extracts from James Thomson's Notebook," *Scottish Art Review,* September, 1889.

———. "James Thomson and his Critics," *National Reformer,* September 15, 1889.

———. *The Life of James Thomson ("B.V.").* London: Reeves and Turner and Bertram Dobell, 1889.

———. *The Life of James Thomson ("B.V.").* Rev. ed. London: Watts and Co., 1914.

———. "Preface" to *The City of Dreadful Night and Other Poems.* London: Watts and Co., 1932.

Schiller, F. C. S. *Must Philosophers Disagree?* London: Macmillan Co., Ltd., 1934.

Sharp, William. "James Thomson," *Encyclopedia Britannica* (9th ed.).

———. "Memoir" in P. B. Marston, *For a Song's Sake, and Other Stories.* London: W. Scott, 1887.

———. *Papers Critical and Reminiscent.* New York: Duffield and Co., 1912.

Shaw, P. E. *The Catholic Apostolic Church.* New York: King's Crown Press, 1946.

Simcox, G. A. "A New Poet," *Fortnightly Review,* July, 1880.

Stedman, E. C. "James Thomson," *Century Magazine,* October, 1887.

Strachey, Lytton. *Queen Victoria.* New York: Harcourt, Brace and Co., 1921.

"The Vision of the Unseen," *Nation,* December 12, 1907.

Wallis, N. H. "James Thomson and his City of Dreadful

Night," in *Essays by Divers Hands,* ed. The Rt. Honorable Earl of Lutton.   London: Oxford University Press, 1935.

Weissel, Josefine.   *James Thomson der Jüngere, sein Leben und seine Werke* (Wiener Beiträge zur Englischen Philologie, XXIV Band.)   Vienna and Leipzig: Wilhelm Braumüller, 1906.

Welby, T. E.   *Back Numbers.*   London: Constable and Co. Ltd., 1929.

"Why James Thomson Did Not Kill Himself," *Spectator,* March 23, 1889.

Woodbridge, B. M.   "A Strange Visitor in the City of Dreadful Night," *Dial,* December 23, 1915.

Zabel, M. D.   "James Thomson's Poems," *Poetry,* July, 1928.

# Index

# INDEX

# INDEX

# INDEX